Michael Hollings

enfolded by christ

an encouragement to pray...

LIVING FLAME PRESS
BOX 74 LOCUST VALLEY, N.Y. 11560

Copyright 1972 by Michael Hollings

SBN 0-914544-10-1

Library of Congress Catalog Card No. 73-84195

Published by
Living Flame Press
Box 74
Locust Valley, N.Y. 11560

Printed in the United States of America

Thanks be to thee, my Lord Jesus Christ, for all the benefits and blessings, which thou hast given to me, for all the pains and insults which thou hast borne for me, O most merciful Friend, Brother and Redeemer; may I know thee more clearly, love thee more dearly, and follow thee more nearly.

Saint Richard of Chichester (died 1255)

Day by day, O dear Lord three things I pray:
to see thee more clearly,
love thee more dearly,
follow thee more nearly,
day by day by day by day.

Contents

Foreword	7
Why I pray	9
Relationship	18
Some mechanics of prayer	35
Petition and intercession	55
Meditation	75
On knowing and knowing about	92
Experience of deeper involvement	100
The Spirit moving among us	117

Foreword

The substance of these pages was originally given in a series of talks to graduates and undergraduates at the Catholic Chaplaincy at Oxford. At the time, they were tape recorded and subsequently edited by Etta Gullick, to whom I am very grateful. A cyclostyled off-print circulated among the students and spread out in different directions. It was used up and reprinted, and part was then reproduced in *Mount Carmel*. Again, various of those who read them wrote or spoke their appreciation, and even asked that the talks in some way be published.

Here is the result, knocked about, edited, cut-down and then added to, but always basically the same.

On the whole, I get fed up with books on prayer, and feel like sighing out: "Oh! Yet another book on prayer!" The only excuse I have, then, for inflicting these pages on you is that they have been useful already over quite a wide area. What God is interested in is the development of the person in relation to himself and all his creation. As one who has experienced the meeting and the message, I am caught up in the longing to do anything which will forward the purpose set out in the letter to the Ephesians chapter 4, verses 12 to 16 including: 'And so . . . we shall become mature men, reaching to the very height of Christ's full stature.'

Now, what you make of this is up to you and the Holy Spirit. But I must thank all those friends (student, teacher, old and young, married and single) who have said: "Teach us to pray." Even more I would thank those who have continued to teach me that I need always to pray, if I am to teach anyone. I cannot name you all, but I love you all, and have no doubt God loves you too. Follow the word of his follower: Let us not love in word or speech, but in deed and in truth.

Southall
Lent 1972   Michael Hollings

Why I Pray

As a personal experience, I would say without hesitation that there is a widespread interest in what makes a person other than oneself 'tick'. Associating as I have done over the years with many going through the later-school and college or university period of life, I have found a large number questioning and questing. For them, it is also a personal quest, but whereas it may be true that other ages have found satisfaction and either guidance or an opening up through a mere theoretical statement, a philosophy and so on, today the existential carries the punch. By that, I mean that the question might have been in other generations phrased in this way: "Why believe?" But now the wording would be more likely to read: "Why do *you* believe?"

This is interesting, because it does not mean that the questioner is particularly interested in me, but there is in me a living, tangible entity, and though I do not profess to know quite what it is that makes the contact, contact does actually seem to be made through the answering of this question.

Now, this is a book which essentially is about prayer, and its concentration is not upon the 'why' of prayer, but much more on the 'how' of prayer. This 'how' has been asked for again and again, and when I have spoken on the subject up and down the British Isles and overseas, I have been quite amazed at the numbers who have been genuinely interested in the 'how'. I suppose, though, that these might well be people who had already gone through at least one phase of the 'why', and so I thought it would be as well to begin at that point, and this in the more personal way.

Why do I pray? The short answer is to the best of my knowledge: "Because my mother prayed." I think that is a very important statement for several reasons. Firstly, I believe it to be true, and to emphasise one of those areas which have been more recently uncovered by those who delve into psychology. From them we learn that the child is influenced not only in the early years of life, but also in the pre-natal period. I understand that it is possible if there is drug-addiction in the parent for this to be present in the very early period of the child's life. I do not think this needs to be heavily underscored, but it can be suggested in a similar way that a nervous mother, a constantly battling partnership, a smooth and happy confinement can all have some effect on the child in the womb . . . and then, of course, there is all the early post-natal period as well.

So that, when I say that I pray because my mother prayed, what I am meaning is that, though I only realise it in hindsight, I have no doubt at all from my later knowledge of my mother that she was a woman who prayed deeply, believed deeply, and lived out her belief in God and man by the love which flowed from her, especially to those poorer than herself. I, therefore, find it impossible to believe that this had no influence on me.

If we take my statement from a very different angle, I expect we can find voices raised in derision, which emphasise other aspects . . . dependence, brain-washing, failure to grow-up, inadequacy. Well, I am prepared to concede any and all of those without being too much upset! This is not the place to argue in this way, but suffice it to say that, very much as an amateur, it seems to me that it is impossible NOT to influence a child, positively or negatively. Those who say that they will leave their children to grow up and make their own decision have an almost impossible task ahead of them.

But enough of that! I went through childhood and into young manhood, taught within a system of Roman Catholic education, disliking it fairly intensely, and emerging with scarcely any knowledge of the 'how' of prayer. Without going into too much detail, World War II had an immense effect on me. I 'fought' through it, loved the companionship and hated the killing; was shattered, disillusioned, lost sight and sound of God, worked only for my fellow men and not for the cause of war, knew what cowardice was in myself, felt my own emptiness and inability to give anyone anything. All this led to the end of the war, and that in turn to further disillusion. The one tangible possibility was fighting for the men for whom I was responsible in the military situation. And then the more I tried, the more inadequate I realised myself to be. This, mind you, was at the age of twenty-two, when men's lives were and had been for several years my responsibility, and now were so in the sense of 'life and death' (I was in Palestine during the beginning of the emancipation of Israel), but also in the sense of developing life . . . future, fiancée, wife, young kids, career, VD and so on.

Therefore, being faced with my post-war life, the futility of killing, the joy of other human beings, the very real and immediate and often intimate concerns of these fellow-men of mine . . . what was the 'how' of my living to be? Quite simply, in statement but not so simply in fact, I needed God and I needed contact with him, so I found my way through again to belief and to prayer. Would it not be likely, however, that, though I certainly did not think of it in this way at the time, I 'went back' to God and prayer, because of the long heritage of my childhood and boyhood? I am immediately reminded of the Christ-parable of the prodigal son, who when all else failed said: "Let me return to my Father's house".

Psychological reasons? . . . yes, I am sure there were, and I am happy if there were, because I am a human being and the God I believe in created the psyche! The rightness and wrongness of different psychological influences and pressures are still very much in the infancy of their discovery, because this is still a young science. This aspect needs to be heeded, but care should be taken not to be 'blinded by science'. There is a vast amount that even the psychologist still does not fully understand definitely in man, if ever he will be able to do so, without recourse to the supernatural.

Once the process has begun I would sometimes feel that I could liken it to drug-addition or alcoholism! The desire to pray can often be a sense of being repelled rather than attracted, only the 'hangover' is pre-prayer, whereas with the other two addictions it is post! The almost nausea can carry on into the prayertime, and even beyond, but despite this the draw to come back for more is insidious. What is more, as with alcohol, the frequency and quantity grow. But, of course, it would be better to liken the process to the development of a relationship of love, which is in truth what it is. As the lover cannot bear to part from the beloved, so the one who 'gets hooked on God' wants to be, consciously or unconsciously, always close to the One, deeply, silently, intently, lovingly, whether in prayer absolute or a prayer-work-service-love relationship.

At least, this is what happened to me. It was at first an urgent seeking inquest of belief, then glimmering, then blinding, then dully, drily dreary. The kaleidoscope of prayer seems infinitely varied, because I personally have not come to the end of the variety. In the beginning, I did an awful lot of work myself, and felt the time given, the tiredness, the battle with sleep, the distractions all worth while—formative, ascetic, fruitful. Regularity begun at this point soon grew into familiarity or routine; but this in turn gave way to a rhythm like breathing which is essential, yet not often realised in day to day living.

And so, for me, over a period of years, the intangible depth which is relationship, friendship, devotion and love all rolled into one has gone on unfolding and enfolding until it has become unthinkable that I should stop living prayer. This is not to say that there is always a clear consciousness of God's loving presence, no time for pain, doubt or further disillusion. All these are possible and part of the variegated pattern. But it does now seem as though to stop praying would be to stop breathing and living all at the same moment.

That is why I pray now, and it follows through from the origin. But there is one aspect which should be mentioned, because it is me and because it is a side which often worries those who find the breakthrough difficult, as a fact in their lives and also because the whole theory appears to them distorted in the light of the gospel of love of neighbour. This aspect is best set out as follows.... It is better to work to and through people, the neighbour, the poor, the oppressed, and in that way you pray most truly. All this airy-fairy business of kneeling down or meditating or thinking you are in personal touch with God doesn't really hold together in this age. The only true prayer is service of your fellow-men!

The reason why I feel I can say something here is because it was the contact with the desire to work for the men and their families with whom I was associated at the end of World War II which drove me to God and prayer in the first place. I would go along, therefore, with anyone who says that this is a way in. But, having realised the need I had through the human need, I came quickly to find the emphasis in my case swinging onto the 'God dimension' as in fact of prior importance.

From this emphasis, in a very practical way, I have found that my small capacity and range of help towards others has extended over and over again. In a fashion which I can only describe as indescribable, both the mind and the heart are opened up. It is embarrassing to talk like this because it sounds so big-headed, but the truth is that I am sure I am not only 'older and wiser', but older and wiser and deeper and more sympathetic, more understanding, more loving, more given and more giving . . . to a degree that I could not foresee, and indeed from which I might have held back had I known what it would mean! Of course, anyone is at liberty to look at me and say: "If that really is what prayer does to a person, then I think he's wasting his time, and I would not bother with it." Right! That may be the witness I give, and if so, I am sorry. But if the witness is different! . . . Someone wrote to me the other day and said how can you give yourself to God in prayer and still remain available at all times to your fellow men . . . how can you walk this tightrope? . . . then it is for you to believe that I am honest and clear-sighted when I say HE has done this in me; it is not a natural growth.

I would, therefore, plead with you to accept that I pray because I am taken up in mankind as well as being caught up in God. After all, it does not take a person of much insight to realise that priestly work, which together with prayer and worship is largely given over to welfare or social work, is normally on the fringes of, if not in the midst of, poverty, disease, death, disaster, squalour, rancour, bitterness, injustice, crime, bewilderment and the rest. Yet life is not just drear, but rather gay; life is not all sorrow and weeping but rather brimming with joy; life is not just falseness and disillusion and despair, but rather vast hope, great truth, deep love.

You see, this is all associated with the Spirit of God and him seen as love. For Saint Paul tells us the effect of the Spirit . . . love, joy, peace, patience and so on. But the Spirit also gives us faith and fortitude, counsel, and understanding, wisdom and the fear of the Lord . . . so many, many things which we need in this day by day living in a world of men and machines, noise and restlessness, extreme riches and extreme poverty. You have to live in this world as much as I do. My question 'Why' to you is: "Why are you reading this book?" And I ask it because I have the answer (I am convinced) which will keep you joyfully walking the tightrope of life in and beyond the nineteen-seventies. But it is an answer which does not seem to be able to be understood by everyone.

It is in some ways summed up in Saint Paul again: "For Christ did not send me to baptise, but to preach the Good News, and not to preach that in terms of philosophy in which the crucifixion of Christ cannot be expressed. The language of the cross may be illogical to those who are not on the way of salvation, but those of us who are on the way see it as God's power to save. . . . Do you see now how God has shown up the foolishness of human wisdom? If it was God's wisdom that human wisdom should not know God, it was because God wanted to have those who have faith through the foolishness of the message that we preach. And so, while the Jews demand miracles and the Greeks look for wisdom, here are we preaching a crucified Christ, to the Jews an obstacle that they cannot get over, to the pagans madness, but to those who have been called, whether they are Jews or Greeks, a Christ who is the power and the wisdom of God. For God's foolishness is wiser than human wisdom, and God's weakness is stronger than human strength." (I Cor 1: 17–25).

There are innumerable Christians who will pay lip service to this exposition. We have to take it to heart and live it, and until we have done this, and felt the outcome in ourselves, we have no right to dismiss it though it may be an obstacle, a madness or a foolishness. This I have found.

Now, that is my personal manifesto in an age when the revitalising of spirituality, the deepening of holiness in Christians and in the Church is *paramount in importance*. Through this development, structures must change; through the change of structures, the climate and freedom must grow which will lead to such spiritual development.

When Christ died, his garment which was won on a lottery by a soldier was seamless. In the present situation, the people of God are a seamless garment. If you try to suggest the unravelling from any one point, you will find that it involves unwinding also in many different areas of the same seamless garment. Similarly, if you try to build the garment from one point you find the weaving involves countless strands. Why do we not admit this, and go ahead with doing 'something beautiful for God'?

> Day by day, O dear Lord three things I pray
> to see thee more clearly,
> love thee more dearly,
> follow thee more nearly,
> day by day by day by day.

Relationship

We all, I imagine, if we have any idea of God at all, must begin at some point wanting to get to know and love him. And most of us most of the time find this getting to know and love him something which is really rather difficult. It would be nice if it came easily to us, but unfortunately it does not. It would be very stupid to make it seem as though it did, because God is 'distant' and he is mysterious, and there are so many things in this world that we are taken up with. I would like you to begin by accepting the fact that the approach to God is not all that easy, and therefore it is something that we have to work away at.

The best way of looking at it, I have always found, is to regard it in the same way as you do a human relationship, but it has got a clear difference. When you are thinking in terms of human relationship, unless you are in someway disorientated or psychologically disturbed, you will quite naturally make relationships with other people. You start off unconsciously with your mother and your father, and then you go on with your friends. Even here, however, there are difficulties, because our personalities do not always meet, and quite frequently you get people who find they are what we would call 'shy'. They have difficulty in communicating even with people who are very close to them and who are in their company all the time. You may be that way yourself, or at least you will certainly know people who are like that. If these people are to develop their means of communication, somebody may well have to help them to do so, because it does not seem to come naturally to them. If they are fortunate they will be helped through their parents; or they may find some friend who does help them by being friendly and drawing them out; or it may be if they get to a stage when they are really completely shut up inside themselves, they will need the assistance of someone else to bring them out, even a psychiatrist.

Now in our relationship with God, perhaps quite unconsciously, if we have been brought up in some way of religion, we have begun to be put in touch with God by our parents. This, however, always takes rather a simple line because we are young. It may be at one stage rather profound for oneself as a child, but it is something that has to grow and develop with our own growth and development. There are stages in this, and it is not by any means something which goes along without the help of other people. So you may be taught to pray quite simply in a verbal sort of way by talking to God, because you are not old enough to think much or to abstract.

People who come to the question of God at a later

stage and who did not know it in their younger days, will perhaps arrive at it in a rather different way. This will be so because when they begin to approach the idea of the existence of God, they will have reached the period of development when they are thinking rather than just talking. Also then they will not be talking to God, as they will not necessarily accept that he exists. What they will be doing is to perform some sort of philosophical exercise on the existence of God. Prayer may well be: "God, if you exist, tell me about yourself."

The ordinary child who has begun by talking to God will also gradually come, one hopes, to think about him. Then, perhaps later, he will come into possession of ideas of God which will be contained within his own mind. They may be drawn from the scriptural picture of Christ or from what is said in scripture. We can develop in very different ways. But a lot of it can remain inside our own intellect and on the whole it is rather seldom that we go very much further than this.

My object is to suggest to you that the ideas about prayer which come in at the first stages are simply not enough. In a human relationship it is not enough just to know John, or know Mary, and to say: "O yes, I know her. I mean I say good morning to her every morning, and we pass the time of day, and yes, I think I know what he or she looks like", and that's it. If you are going to develop a human relationship into anything verging on love or eventually coming to love, the knowledge has got to be much closer and more intimate than that. And the question that I want to raise with you at this point, because we are going on through it, is whether I, that's you, individually get further in prayer than treating God to some extent as an object to be talked at, rather than as a real person.

I do not want you to get all muddled up with philosophical ideas of what one means by person, I mean here a real person who can be communicated with in a deeply intimate way following the pattern of human relationship. This implies that sometimes one will be speaking directly to, sometimes one will be thinking about, sometimes one will be looking at, and sometimes one will be silent with. There will be all these different combinations. Sometimes one will simply become aware of God, without even realising that one is in communication with him. There are deeper ways that one comes to, but there is a great variety because as human beings we continue to be varied, and we do not remain at a particular pitch or level at every moment of our daily existence.

Here I would like to say that we are human. Therefore, we have our minds and bodies, and we have all the human surroundings that we live in, and it is within this framework that God expects us to make our relationship with him. If we try to do something which is completely unnatural, then we are likely to go pop at some point. Some people have been known to force themselves through violent asceticism into rather unnatural forms of communication with God. This, however, is not something which is advocated by the church, though there is a place for self-discipline and a place also for asceticism, doing without, penance and so on. These are not very popular things at the present time, but still necessary in relation to God. This happens in exactly the same way that you may need to be somewhat ascetic in your relation to your girl friend or your boy friend, particularly if they either want you to stay up very late in the night or get you up very early in the morning to go mountain climbing or something like that. You will have to see what you can do about this and whether it will break your love or whether it is worth getting up that early or whether it is worth while waiting that long—whatever it may be. And so with God, asceticism does have a place. But we are, to start with anyhow, in this natural realm of being an ordinary human person with a mind and a body. We are liable to all the human distractions that anybody else is liable to, and these are not things that are going simply to pass out of our lives when we get in touch with God.

Again, if you will perhaps forgive me constantly coming back to the question of human relationship, you may be very fond of somebody, and your mind may be on that person, and then something cataclysmic may happen; for example, your tutor or boss tells you that if you do not do better you will fail your exams or lose your job. Then all of a sudden, although he or she is very close to your heart, the question of your future looms rather large and next time you see your friend you are not terribly interested in him or her, you are constantly talking about what is going to happen to you. Therefore you could call this, when you are in their presence, a distraction. Indeed if you get too caught up in it, the other party may get extremely irate with you and want you to get back to your old self somehow, and may even lose sympathy with you.

So in relation to God these distractions are going to be there, and the level of our communication with him is going to vary. Now because of this, there are various techniques which are applicable to our development in prayer, and one has to distinguish between techniques and prayer itself. In a sense many of the things that have come up as Christian and non-Christian practice with regard to the development of prayer, are techniques. Vocal prayer, for instance is a technique because it uses what we have in order to bring us into contact with God who in our belief is in fact already in contact with us. But it is one way in which our human nature is reassured that there can be a contact, because this speaking is something natural which we can do. Also thinking or meditating are a part of our natural function. When we are dealing with a human being, we want to think about that human being. In the same way with God we can very definitely set ourselves to think about him, so that we can become to some extent learned in the knowledge of God. Again it is something which is not itself necessarily prayer; it may simply be getting the background to our discovery of God.

Similarly, it can be very useful for us to pray in a particular posture, and this again is very natural. Part of prayer should certainly be adoration when we can sense something of the immensity of God, and feel a need to adore him. And there is something which perhaps is not always liked, but which is fitting, about kneeling, because it does somehow put you in a state of physical adoration before God. It could be that at another stage you found standing or sitting was more convenient. Orientals like people to sit upright with a straight line down the spine. These are techniques, which are only techniques.

There are also ways, which I shall discuss later on, of developing something of a more perfect consciousness of God by using ejaculatory prayer throughout the day. In this way we can keep ourselves, very mechanically perhaps, but somehow close to the presence of God. These things, which are very varied, are for the individual to choose, and it is very difficult in a sense, to lay down what any particular individual ought to do unless one is dealing directly with him. What I really want to stress is that there is an enormous variety in the approach to God, or, to put it in the words of Saint John of the Cross: "No two men go more than half-way on the same road to God."

There are, however, pointers and suggestions that can be given. To some extent each of us goes the same way as other people for a certain length of time and there are common experiences, but by and large, because this is *your* contact and development with God, it is something that is very personal to *you*. I am talking here about your personal prayer, not general public worship which is another field.

Now it is true to say when I speak to a group of people whom I know, and who, to some degree, know each other, that I do not have the same relationship with each person, because each person is individual. In a sense I am able to have a contact, a friendship, with each person, and for me, to some extent the relationship remains constant in so far as this is 'me' having a relationship. But it also has its variety because it is towards different people. And each individual's relationship back to me is quite different to that of the person next to him. Also the relationship of people sitting next to each other will be different again from their's with me, but yet there will be something common in it. But if someone comes and tells me that so-and-so is proving very difficult because each time he talks to her she seems to back away, what is the reason for this? Then I have all sorts of possible suggestions of what it might be that drives her away, but in the end my questioner has to find his own way through in that relationship, because nobody can do more than make suggestions to help him.

So indeed it is with God, but outside suggestions,

nevertheless, are extremely valuable in this, and I would think that probably in the Catholic church anyway at the present time this is not sufficiently stressed. We can and should help each other in prayer. It is not just that the priest helps you, but you yourselves individually can help each other. This is done sometimes by forming prayer groups, or by one individual who is known to be interested helping another individual and so on. It is something which is a Christian responsibility and not simply one for the priests.

Well now, this as you can see is all very vague and general, and it is meant to be at this stage because we do start vaguely and generally. So I will go back to the very beginning, to the question which is very much in the air at the present time, and which which I almost began to touch on in the question of personal prayer: that is as to whether or not we can in fact have contact with a personal God, in a personal way. There has been quite a lot written and said indicating that this is no longer the way, and some people suggest that the whole effort must be to find God in your neighbour and in that way to work out your salvation. And your only valid prayer, therefore, is in a sense a prayer in community when you are working for your neighbour. This is a very absolute way of putting it and I do not think that it is valid.

The other thing is that there are basically two methods of approach. In the first way you go straight to God, person to person, and then come from God to your neighbour. The proponents of this way say: "now you are here, you have the great commandment which is firstly to love God, and secondly to love your neighbour as yourself"; you do the God-motion first and that leads on to the neighbour. The current idea very much put forward today is that this is a getaway from the reality of existence. Those who follow the second way tell us that you must go first to your neighbour, and from this going to your neighbour you will then move up to God. And they put forward passages from the gospels like the one in Saint Matthew (Matt. 22: 39) where we are told love of neighbour sums up the whole of the law; or other passages such as 'if you say you love God whom you cannot see and you do not love your neighbour whom you do see, what is the value of it?' (1 John 4:10)

From my point of view, and this is completely autobiographical. my way was by having lost my faith for some time; finding that in working for my neighbour and trying to work with him and serve him, I was so inadequate that I was forced back to believing in God. And for that reason, therefore, at that stage it certainly was true for me that I worked through my neighbour and found God. But once having found God, it has seemed to me ever since that the basic thing that is important is the discovery of God and development of the relationship with God and from there to go back to the neighbour. I would say that both these ways are perfectly valid. I think it depends on the individual which way he or she finds it goes better.

However, neither of these ways is valid unless the triangle (God, me, my neighbour) is completed. The danger of going directly to God is that we can become, as it were, spiritually selfish and in that sense we shall never penetrate the depths of God's love and so we may easily become frustrated about all this. And if our love of God does not carry us out to our neighbour, we shall certainly be unfulfilled, because we cannot truly love God directly in this way without the overflow which goes to our neighbour. It simply is not valid. But unfortunately it can sometimes happen that we do not overflow, and so in one way or another it is a counterfeit, done perhaps in all goodness, but nevertheless it is a counterfeit, in which somehow the world is neglected because God is so seemingly directly in the centre.

In the second way the danger is that it will just be straight humanism, where the only thing that matters is our neighbour. And though theoretically we should be finding God in our neighbour, in point of fact we seem to stick at our neighbour, and we do not bring God into it in any way, and God does not grow in us at all. This, I think, you can see happening. It may well be when such a person gets to the gates of heaven, God will say: "Well done, I was in fact in your neighbour all the time, so here we are." But this is not quite what I was trying to get at when I spoke of the development of the direct relationship with God by going through the neighbour, which is certainly possible.

To turn to another point about the relationship to God in prayer, one would think that unless one actually believed in God the whole of this process would seem to be something of a nonsense. I do not think it is complete nonsense for I know people, and I think that there are many people about in this world, who really would like to believe that there is a God, but are shy of beginning to make any probe out towards him, or think that they will be hypocritical if they do in fact begin that probe. If you or any friends are in that stage, then somehow or other the step should be made to an opening to God. It can be a cry for help. It can be as distant as: "God if you exist, teach me about yourself" or something of this sort. But the basis of our prayer, whether we believe or do not believe, in some sense is faith. And one does not know quite how faith begins, but it seems obvious it begins from God, and it seems obvious that we, perhaps, at some stage or other have to put ourselves into the way of it. A silly statement of this is, that the only way of making an act of faith is to make an act of faith—and that in itself is something of a leap in the dark in which we do not really know what we are doing. It may, however, be necessary to start in that way.

After this first leap in the dark, faith is constantly present in whatever level of prayer we get to and in whatever depth of relationship we reach. If I may switch back to the human relationship again, even when you marry someone and you feel as though you have got as close as you can to that person, so that you are prepared to pledge yourself to him or her for a lifetime, you are still making an act of faith to some extent, for you still have not completely penetrated that human individual and moreover you never will penetrate that individual completely. Besides this, that individual is going to go on growing throughout the rest of life. In the same way in our advancement in the knowledge and love of God, this faith has to be here, not only because we continue to develop but also because in a certain sense God goes on developing in relation to us. By that I mean we are the ones that are developing but there is this growth in us of the knowledge of God which, just because it is a growth in knowledge of God, is also a growth in the understanding of our ignorance of God. We get this development of closeness to him combined with the element of distance from him, which is very much a matter of living still in faith, because sometimes the distance from him is quite overwhelmingly greater than any sense or knowledge of closeness to him. So faith is enormously important the whole way.

Finally one needs to go from where one is. If more than one person reads this, it can be guaranteed that each will be in a different situation with regard to prayer life, and therefore in a very different situation with regard to whether anything I have said has any meaning. That is good and as it should be. It is essential to realise that prayer life is something which must go on developing. It is not something that anyone has achieved to any perfection here. I am only writing from an amateur's point of view, from some little knowledge I have of it from personal experience, from reading, from talking, and so on. It is rather like this when first you are deeply in love. You will say: "I know what love is"; but I think if you talk to a Darby and Joan who are in their eighties or nineties, and have been married fifty or sixty years, they will say: "Well, perhaps you do, but wait another fifty years and then you'll know what love is." Prayer is rather like this. This is in a sense what is so marvellous about it, and this is what is so sad when people do not go forward in prayer and grow in this relationship, but feel instead that the whole thing is a washout.

We have to start from where we are, and there is a certain sense in which we are see-sawing in prayer all the time. The person who is most deeply involved in God is still making little ejaculations of love, or saying the Lord's Prayer or whatever it may be, and the person who is just beginning may have moments of being caught up into something which is without words and without anything except an impression of love and a sense of experience. So we are all together in this, and it is a great experience. To put oneself in its way, to open oneself to it—this is very demanding, but very worthwhile. So do not wait! Try it now!

Q We can feel ourselves talking to God, but how does he reply to us?

Very simply, I must say straight away that he does not reply as you sit there by something that is automatically and immediately clear to your own mind like somebody's words. It is not ordinarily like this, though it can be, and people have experienced it this way. But the main way that the word of God has been given to us is through the development of the gospels, through the scriptures and through the Old Testament. Therefore here is a source, but as with any source book it is a question of whether your mind is open, orientated and trained to some sort of understanding. This, therefore, might seem to be difficult as it might appear that you need to be a trained scripture scholar or something like this before God will really speak to you. But this is not so, for in fact he can speak through scripture, in the straight message of scripture, in a way that perhaps would seem woefully wrong to a scripture scholar but, which nevertheless I think, has a real validity in personal development.

If you pursue the relationship by talking to him, by thinking of him, and by reading about him and sometimes oddly enough by listening to sermons where you may get a good point, then what does happen is that in a certain way you become sensitive. And if you become sensitive in the right way it can be that God speaks to you more and more, in more and more different ways, because if you are, somehow, more aware of him and his presence and so on, then (I'm very bad at trying to describe this) everything that happens seems to radiate God. You get the Hopkins' line: "The world is full of the glory of God." You know it just is! It is not that if you wake up in the morning and it is a most beautiful morning, you say just "Ah!" but somehow it's "Ah, God!", for he is in it as it were. Obviously this can be carried to excess and sound very whimsical. On the other hand if you suffer a loss or something like that, it is very difficult. Here is just one personal experience. Some time ago a nice woman who had spent Christmas with us had a stroke and she was in hospital. I rang up another woman who also had Christmas with us and told her about this, and she said: "Oh, no, how awful," so I said: "Well now you pray; I think it would be marvellous if she died tonight." She said: "Oh, no, surely not; we must pray for her to get better." I said: "No, it would be wonderful if she died tonight," and I am glad to say she did. God and I agreed!

There is a sense in which you can now and then take a view which seems to be completely opposite to the worldly one. You can sometimes get a sense out of something which seems very different. Then in this, there grows a silence in your prayer, which I do not think we can describe very well. All I can say is that out of this silence there come all sorts of understandings which on one level, unfortunately for us, we do not always realise we understand or even know. It is as deep as that. We will talk about that at a later stage. A way of summing it up perhaps is to say that the varieties of ways in which God can talk to you is pretty well numberless, once you have begun to get on his wavelength as it were. It might be rather as though you had a foreign language like French, of which like me you have only a very little smattering. So you hear an extraordinary burble of sound coming out of someone's mouth. It is really quite unintelligible. And then if you go to France occasionally like me, you begin to hear one or two odd words and they begin to mean something to you. Gradually, of course, if you become fluent, you come to understand the way they tick and that they are saying something. Possibly getting on to God's wavelength is something of that sort.

Q What is the role of emotion in prayer?

This is very much underlining that you are a human being, as I was trying to say. In the ordinary course of events a human being ought not to be totally unemotional. I am sure a doctor, for example, would tell me that there ought to be emotions in a human being—they are all part of us, aren't they? So if one is being brought out properly, the emotions are going to be validly used by God. But the point to stress is that one must not be dependent on one's emotions. This again would surely link up with human love, and quite a lot of human love is keeping going, almost with the will. You do in some way love this person—you know you do—but at the present moment all you can do is just keep going with him. So one ought not to expect too much from the emotions or depend too much on them.

On the other hand, I do not think that one simply wants to cut them out. It is difficult because one must have a balance. There again it will vary from person to person. But in the variety of prayer there are times when one feels like singing Hallelujah! I do not see why you should not have a David today dancing in front of the Ark and that sort of thing. It is tremendous, and even some of our liturgy is getting like this. This is alright. The trouble comes when emotion has to be forced. You get people who literally have the gift of tears. They just cannot contain their tears. It is not a weeping of sorrow or anything necessarily, it can be just sheer joy. There are other times when you can really be taken up, and humanly you can too. In ordinary human events you can be taken up in the sorrow and pain of the world. This can happen in prayer in a way which is pretty inexplicable, but you just do suffer. One might say you are just being emotional about it, but no, I think this has a very real place in prayer. But if you thought you could judge your prayer by how you reacted emotionally, then I would think you were barking up the wrong tree.

Q Could emotion be a distraction?

There are all sorts of different approaches to this. I think we could be distracted by emotion. We could also be distracted by trying to get rid of emotion, if you see what I mean. But I should think the distraction of emotion is much more when you are wanting to rely on it. However, it is certainly true also that if you live a life of prayer, a lot of it is going to be entirely unemotional; it is going to be done with the will, putting yourself there, being fairly empty and blank. I am afraid humanly speaking we look for consolations or something of this sort in prayer. This can be the cause of tremendous distraction, because we feel: "Well, goodness me, I have been sitting here for half an hour and it has been absolute hell, and unless something happens soon. . . ." And one can get terribly emotionally involved in that way. That is just a distraction—and we must go on emptily, not expecting God to intervene with a vision or an emotional boost. And so emotion can be a distraction if we come to expect it or to wallow in it: it can also be a distraction in its absence, if we feel aggrieved at not feeling, and allow ourselves self-pity or a struggle to achieve an emotional stimulus.

Some mechanics of prayer

This chapter covers the various mechanics of prayer and is very basic. What I am trying to get round to and lead you on to, and urge you forward to, is a much deeper form of relationship with God. But first I am going to set the course and get a general sense of discipline. I will begin with the ascetics of prayer, but will go on to the ordinary types of prayer. This is useful not only for your own development, but it should also be of use to you in helping other people when they talk to you about prayer. It is one of our Christian duties that we should be able to lead others on, to help them and tell them how to pray, and it is something that any Christian ought to be able to do.

It is very important to understand that the development of prayer is a very personal thing, and therefore insights that you may have, may possibly lighten some of the difficulties of another person.

People's difficulties and insights can vary considerably. This is why it is useful to talk to others about prayer, and to listen to experience which may be different from your own.

The first thing I would like to get on to is the need for discipline in the prayer life. I do not want to make you feel that it is desperately hard, but I would suggest that discipline is part of the general way of our living, though perhaps I am wrong about this. However, it would seem to me that anybody who is going to get anywhere in life, unless he or she is totally brilliant, and I am afraid this is not the case with most of us, has to have a certain amount of discipline. I do not believe that pictures just get painted. I do not believe, on the whole, people just turn into wonders in the world of music, that it just happens to them. They have to practise regularly and hard. I do not believe that books just get written in a flash overnight. It does not happen that way. There is a very real need for discipline, and this applies to prayer as well.

If I come back again to my usual analogy of ordinary human relationships, anybody knows that for a relationship to grow there is a tremendous need for discipline in it. A discipline is needed in the development because we must be regular, and this is the fundamental point for me. I would put it as the very cornerstone of all prayer life that it must be regular. Now I do not intend to lay down exactly what I mean by regular, because here again it depends on the individual. But the church has traditionally indicated, for example, the need for morning and night prayers. And this sums up that it is important for us to be in touch, in communication, in relationship with God every single day of our lives. I am not saying that it is not possible to have a relationship with God or a fellow human being at a much greater interval. Of course it is, but if you want to maintain and develop a really deep relationship either with God or with man, it has got to be something more regular than just infrequent. Here you have something that is fundamental. If you cannot take that, I really do not think that you are going to advance very far in the prayer life. As with a personal relationship, the more you realise this, the more obvious it becomes. And once you have begun to realise this, you may find that you have not always the will to live up to it. But once you have come to realise it, then the problem is that God almost seems to take up too much time and to be too central in your life. You can even get to a funny stage when you get a detachment from the world, but we need not talk about this now. It is the regularity that I want to stress here.

I will now be more specific, though the stress may appear to be on pernickety little points. First of all let us look at discipline as far as the body is concerned, for we must remember that we are made up of body and soul. The body has its place in our communication with God. We are whole people and we worship him with body and soul. The body is responsible for a lot of our condition. It is certain that after having had an extremely good wining and dining, we can be in a fairly meditative mood, but whether it is a godly meditation or whether it is simply rather soporific, is left to your imagination if it is still working at that time! So Henry Suso says: "He who wishes to catch a slippery eel by the tail, and he who wishes to serve God with a pampered and soft body, both deceive themselves." It just cannot be done. A certain asceticism is necessary.

This does not necessarily mean that you have to

do all sorts of bodily mortifications. These have gone out of fashion at the present time, and for the ordinary course of development I do not want to suggest that you go in for any bodily mortifications in that way. But there is the question of control, which can affect eating and drinking, and particularly the question of sleeping. This again ties up with the regularity, because as it seems to me, and again this is an individual thing, somewhere or another if you understand the need to be alone with God, you have to find a time to be alone with God.

And in the course of my life, I have certainly found that the best time to be alone with God, as a single person, is early in the morning, simply because not everyone else likes getting up early in the morning or bothers you at that particular time. Also, if you are living in a student community you never know what time you are going to get to bed, so if you leave your time to be alone with God to when night time comes, you can be very easily disillusioned. Besides, you know yourselves, once you get going on a day, things fill up, unless you are determined to fit something in. In conjunction with this there arises the question of how much sleep you need and how you are going to regulate this, and so on. This is one of the penances, one of the asceticisms, which can be suggested. However, I won't go into all the possible types of penance that may come in.

One of the bodily things that is important is to try to develop a stillness in yourself. "Be still and know that I am God." You could take that as a watchword for the development of prayer. The peculiarity of it is that sometimes when you are trying to give yourself to prayer you get into an enormous state of fidget. I suppose this happens partly because it is rather unnatural to sit still, and we do tend to get jumpy with distractions and so on.

This brings us on from bodily to mental discipline. I will touch on this again later. There were some questions about distractions in the last chapter. The mental discipline is that we are trying to concentrate on God. The difficulty of mental discipline is that, on the whole, the mind, whether it is well-trained or not, is always going to have distractions. Now I mean distractions; the main thing, I am quite certain, is that we have them as background noise and we should not concentrate even to remove them.

Take the example of a person living or working in a room overlooking a noisy street, or a person living on the fly-in route to a busy airport. If such a person concentrates on the noise, and says it is impossible to begin a conversation or put pen to paper until the noise ceases or the airport is closed —well, he will never get going, and will probably end up in a mental home or dead from frustration. If, however, he accepts the noise, he will gradually forget it, concentrate through or 'underneath' it, without fuss or more than mild disturbance.

Also it pays to envelop yourselves in God in the day so that the things distracting us are actually coming into our prayer as things already mentioned and talked about with God. If as we go about, we begin with the practice and grow into the habit of 'taking God with us,' we fall naturally into referring things to him. It would only be a stupid person who could imagine that twenty-three and a half hours a day spent without much reference to God and piled high with the busy clutter of the world could all be excluded by an act of the will during half an hour of prayer. After that length in the world of noise and effect we cannot hope to disappear into a cocoon of silence where we can worship God in peace, detached. No, no! This would not be human prayer, which involves the whole of us, and is a growth from and into reality, not a flight from it.

What is more important in the mental discipline, and this will be dealt with later, is that we have to go beyond the mind. We have to accept the fact that God is beyond the mind. The mind is too small. And the mind, for this reason, becomes fidgety, just as the body becomes fidgety, because it cannot hold God. Therefore it does not enjoy or rest in him. If we can come to accept that God is 'beyond' (by which I mean greater than and so inexpressible) then one of the things that we ought also to accept is that God is not dependent on our distractions and that what he needs from us is something in the way of attention, and particularly attention of the will. The mind does not like this, I think, because it is being put in a corner and it 'feels ignored'. God is not ignoring it, he is simply using the other methods that he has, particularly that he can come to one without consciously using the ordinary methods of which we are conscious.

This you have to take as a matter of faith, for I am quite certain that it is true, and I think if you have this understanding, it is something which will be very helpful to you. I can describe it by comparing it to the subliminal advertisement which is flashed on the screen in such a way that you do not know you have even seen it. Now in prayer you can be concentrating, but perhaps what you are concentrating on is not the message that is being given to you. Sometimes you feel you are concentrating on your distractions, but in fact what you have come to prayer wanting to do is to concentrate on God. In what I am suggesting to you, namely that you are with your will wanting to concentrate on God, when in fact you are thinking about supper, there is no reason why God should not 'come in under', as it were, to enlighten you without you even realising it, so that at a later stage you say: "I wonder where that came from?"

The mental discipline also needs to be backed up, and backed up fairly continually, with the steady acquisition of knowledge of God which comes largely through reading. You cannot necessarily read very profoundly or very long, but I am sure it is necessary to have something by you to read. And in this I would want to stress with you that part of the discipline, just like learning how much sleep you need, is learning to take and make use of the odd couple of minutes or five minutes with which each of our days is littered. Sometimes we have a tendency to feel that this is not worth doing unless it can be done for half an hour or so. Surely you have to make every odd minute available to yourself! Never travel in a train without a book, never go up the street without a book.

I used to infuriate people when I was an army officer because I always had a book under my arm instead of a swagger stick—they said it was the wrong form of dress, but lying in a slit trench you can read a book rather better than you can wave a stick about. You would be surprised how much you can get through when you have a book with you all the time and how much time you can waste if you don't. Don't ever say: "I am not the sort of person who can read in a train". You may not be able to read when the train is moving, but trains are always stopping, in this country anyhow, so you may get plenty of opportunity to read!

You must persevere. One of the dangers that we come up against, and one of the frustrations, is that the whole thing is so empty. We are not getting anywhere: I have tried; it does not work. What is the good? Is it real anyway? Is it not a waste of time?—You have got to go on. You have got to persevere. You have got to be regular. You have got to do it, day in and day out.

The knowledge of your closeness to God, does in fact come. I assure you it comes. When you have practised it as long as I have—perhaps some of you have practised it longer—then you will be able to say: "You were right after all!"

It is this point that I came to in the last chapter. Faith is the air which prayer breathes. As I said about distractions, you have got to have faith that God is still with you and in contact with you and working on you. So when nothing happens at all, when you are not even in a darkness, or a coldness or anything else, but it is just grey and empty, you must have faith. When there is no return, or it does not pay off, or whatever phase you may use to express your disillusion, you will have to have faith and go on with giving your time and yourself to prayer.

And now, a final aspect of this. I would call it allowing yourself, being disciplined in yourself, to be 'pickled in God'. By that I mean that you accept God around you, in you, penetrating you and conditioning you. In one way you are willing to be passively impregnated by God, and believe this is going on, even when there is little or no evidence that this is the case. Or you can take the other idea of the leaven—that you let God leaven the whole of your being—a process which begins by the discipline of pushing God into your day.

The most important part of what we have to do in this leavening process, is to make certain, even fairly mechanically, that we are coming to him, that he is consciously with us at periods of the day which we would not normally associate with God at all. Why? So that you will associate that period of the day with God. Quite simple! Just opening yourself up to the fact that what you are supposed to believe (I don't know if you do) is that God is with you day and night, day in and day out, year in and year out. There is never a moment in your life when God is not present with you. Now this is the becoming aware, the acceptance of living in the atmosphere of God, the being leavened by God, the being pickled in God, whatever you like to call it—something that will catch your imagination so that in fact you live that way.

A rather different theme, but all tying up with the same basic mechanics, namely what sort of posture should one have in prayer? I am sure the answer is that you suit yourself. There may be times when one seems more suitable than another. If you are really in adoration, you may like to lie flat on your face, or perhaps kneeling may be the right sort of posture. However, usually you cannot lie flat on your face in a church or people will wonder what you are doing! If you feel kneeling is the right posture for you, then kneel. I fancy in earlier days people made rather a thing of kneeling, particularly in private prayer, and it was almost an ascetic practice that one knelt and knelt and knelt. It can be very good from that point of view, but it can be a total distraction.

Some people find standing enormously helpful. It can certainly be so if you are inclined to go to sleep, though it is possible to go to sleep standing up as well as sitting down! The early Christians used to stand, and we have now taken again to standing in the presence of God. It is an old way of praying and it has got a lot behind it, and it is certainly worth thinking about. It is not something that is greatly practised among us at the moment, but it is worth trying if you have not already. I personally like sitting and believe in sitting. I don't think it is just laziness. I think there is something relaxed about sitting and, at the same time, provided you are not just sitting all folded up as it were, there is a certain form to it as well as a certain relaxation. I find this good, and probably a lot of people do as well. Of course it has similarities with Eastern religious postures, though theirs is a rather less supported way than the way I would sit.

Lying is extremely good provided that it is done in a sensible manner and is not simply a matter of going to sleep. But do honestly think in terms of this because people do not always realise that relaxing and letting go has to do with prayer. For prayer is not meant to be a tremendous tension all the time, but to be quiet and relaxed in the atmosphere of God, to feel at home with him. The question to ask yourself and to answer by practical experiment is what way you may feel openly free, relaxed—just simply from the physical and psychological point of view. This is a form of relaxation which would be recommended to you no doubt by a psychiatrist, if you yourself were very tense. Well, this has all got something to do with one's relationship with God because it is in this sort of state that you are liable to be more open to God, and perhaps less conscious of the barriers and so on. I suppose it has a likeness to the psychiatrist's couch; it has a similarity of purpose. However, on the other hand if you are lying down it is quite possible just to drop off to sleep!

Breathing and things like this have a part to play in prayer if you find them useful. I do not see why anything that is natural should not be of use in relating to God, for our union with him makes us more fully human. I do not think drugs are helpful whatever is claimed for them in the realm of perception. They have nothing to do with prayer because our approach has to be natural not drug-induced. I do think the kind of relaxation that can be got by steady rhythmical breathing, or something of this sort, may help people to still themselves and become mentally calm, and in that way open themselves to God. If this is helpful, if it can be combined with some ejaculation or aspiration, then I am sure that this is something useful and can be used.

In all these things, it is helpful to have someone to guide you. If you don't, there is no one, unless you have a friend to talk to, against whom you may spark off and say: "This is what I do, do you think it is a good thing?" As a priest, I often talk to people about prayer and meet the sort who say that when it is cold at night that they jump into bed, curl up and say their prayers there. This may simply mean that they go straight to sleep. They do not really say their prayers at all. If someone said to me openly: "I find the best way of praying is to get into a nice warm bed with an electric blanket, and I find that I am caught up by God in no time", I might begin to wonder whether they might not have a slightly more ascetic practice. Whereas they might go on kidding themselves that they were in a state of complete nocturnal illumination. So it is useful to have someone to spark off on and to tell you what they think about what you are doing.

Just as I suggested that you could find odd minutes for reading if you took a book around with you, so I think it should be stressed that you are not confined to praying at a time when you are alone with God in your room or in church. You can pray any time and anywhere, and it is very important to realise this. The more disciplined you become about this, the more likely you are to pray at any time, anywhere. Glancing at God is something that is enormously important at different times. Buses, trains, any incident that may occur, any person you may meet, these are all opportunities afforded for such glancing if you are living in the sort of atmosphere where you are God-conscious. Moving from one place to another, in an odd five minutes, can give an admirable chance for five minutes with God if you want it that way. Equally well, if you have five minutes before a meal or while waiting to catch a bus, then use it—don't waste it.

At first, and I have to re-emphasise this, it all seems very mechanical, it all seems extraordinary in a sense. Is it really necessary to make it all as complicated as this? The answer is that it is like learning to drive a car. When you are preparing for your test you have the Highway Code, all the hand signals, and you are so busy thinking of all these things that in a sense you cannot enjoy driving as you are concentrating on whether you are doing the right things. At a later stage when the whole process has become part of your routine, you no longer think of it because you do it automatically. Well, it is rather like this as regards God and the concentration on him. You have built up a kind of way of living and breathing which is a way of living prayer.

I will say one or two things very briefly on vocal prayer. Again it is important to start making it regular. We tend to think of vocal prayer as being the first type of praying, but I do not believe that the types of prayer fit into water-tight compartments. My whole theory, practice and experience is that the thing flows in and out the whole time. I maintain very strongly that there will never be a time when you will cease using vocal prayer. You will, I hope, go on with your vocal prayer in one way or another right until the day you die. If you are conscious as you are dying you may very well die saying "Jesus" or "Christ have mercy on me a sinner", because it is normal for you to use this prayer day by day. If it has not been your practice you may die with the latest pop song on your lips or anything, even expletives.

It depends how you have lived, I think, because my experience of watching people die, die consciously, is that what comes out of them at that time very much comes out of the centre spirit of the life they have lived. If one looks at it from the long term, this of course is why one wants to have people living toward God, because the saying 'happy is the death of a saint' is so very true. To see a holy person die is really a remarkable thing. I am quite certain from what I have seen that the peace and sense of God is something which one would want for anybody one loved.

To return to vocal prayer, Christ himself starts by telling us about the Lord's prayer. The disciples asked to be taught how to pray because they had seen him praying, and had seen something of the attraction of his prayer. So he gave them the very simple 'Our Father'. I would say here is a model prayer, and it is one that is used frequently in our public worship of God, and no doubt will be one that all of you use during your own private prayer. The 'Our Father' and the prayers of saints, and all these things are in a sense models, but they are not necessarily the direct expression that you would want to say to God. Your words should spring from the way you yourself address a person.

The ordinary example I give is if you are going to approach somebody and want to get on with him. You may, I suppose, if you read a lot, find some speech from Shakespeare and go and hold it in front of him and let forth at him in Shakespeare's words. However, I doubt very much if you are going to make much contact if you do that. Your friend might say: "Come off it, now that's Shakespeare, what about you? I am not terribly interested in him; I can go and read him any time." This may sound silly. But you see what I am saying here is what I have learnt about prayer.

I could quote from far better books than I could write myself. I could extensively quote scripture, the fathers of the church, modern writers, the mystics—but these would not be my personal experience in prayer. If you want what they said, please read them. If you want to read me, then you have me. What we tend to say to God is: "Here am I, and I am now going to give you Saint Bernard's prayer because after all Saint Bernard knew how to talk to you." It seems ridiculous in a sense. It may be that you feel this expresses your inner feelings in regard to God, and sometimes it may do. Some of the verses of the Psalms, and some prayers can really get us somewhere and lift us up above our own puny thoughts. But still, one wonders really!

For Saint Valentine's Day do you buy a great and beautiful Valentine which has got some wonderful words inside it, or do you make a little daub on a bit of paper and write your own personal message in disguised writing? Which is the more effective? I don't know. But I think I would probably opt for the personal message. I think it is much better that you should say: "Come off it, God," or something like that, rather than use high falutin' phrases and so on. If you really want to see, say as they did in the gospel, "Lord that I may see". If you have not got any faith say, "Lord, increase my faith". If you feel like it, say "God, I am utterly fed up; my girl friend's gone away, I have had a rotten day at work and I didn't sleep much last night; it is absolute hell". This is the most expressive sort of prayer that you can have. Another day you may be able to say, "It is just marvellous, the sun is shining, there is spring in the air, and I have just had a letter from my best friend", and then it is literally 'Alleluia!' There is nothing else you want to say! It is not particularly your word, but it simply seems to come out. This is the way I think that prayer should develop.

Well then, it does not have to be a long set prayer and it does not have to be something which is constantly new. I suppose we get bored with our prayers, but God does not. God simply wants to know that we want to know him, that we want to love him, and so on. He also wants to know what we want. He does know, but it is still good that we communicate, as it were. This is right if we feel that this is what we want to do, and I am talking now of the stage or the period when we are not able to go any further, particularly when we are tired and want to hold on to something and you really may just have to say, "Lord, Lord, Lord", or "Help" or something of this sort. It may be that you have simply a verse of a psalm, for example "Out of the depth", or anything that seems to you at that moment to be expressive. It may be that this will be the basic prayer you use for perhaps a day, a week, a month, a year. It may be that it is "My Lord and my God", and that nothing else seems to be any good at all.

You may be able to get something out of some of the great long prayers, some sort of readings from scripture, lovely verses from the psalms, but you must come back to "My Lord and my God"— that's all and that's it. Well, wonderful! And God does not get bored with it. If this expresses you to God then that is all that matters. You are trying to communicate with him. That is why practices like the Jesus prayer of the Orthodox Church have been so popular. And in the past, of course, though in a slightly different way, the rosary has proved to be remarkable. It uses the hands, and to some extent quiets the mind. It has this steady repetition and it does have a certain rhythm to it, all of which opens communication between you and God.

However, eventually of course, in this communication, at certain times anyhow you get into silence. Though I am talking about vocal prayer and about the fact that it will continue until you die, I do not mean to say that it is a non-stop monologue by you. But simply at some time in your life, right away through until you die, probably at some time every day if once you get into the habit of being with God in prayer, you will have some form of vocal communication which may be fairly continuous. If you are sick, or if you are in a state of worry, if your mind is in a turmoil, this may be the only way that you can keep a contact with God. At another time when you are still and you are knowing God in stillness, there may not be any need for vocal prayer at all. But I do believe that it does in fact continue throughout life.

Q Would you enlarge on what you said about discipline with regard to sleep?

In what I have just said I have linked up the question of sleep with discipline. In our lives it is interesting to know what we need in the way of sleep. When some crisis comes along we are quite ready to go without sleep and, my theory rightly or wrongly and the way I tend to live, is that we can sleep and should sleep basically for a period of time. But in a sense the more you sleep the more you want to sleep, and the more sleep you seem to need. I am not a doctor and cannot lay things down but I imagine people's requirements with regard to sleep do vary. However, I fancy that there is a margin within which we can try ourselves out on this and see what we need in the way of sleep. This clearly must fit into one's pattern of life.

My pattern of life would be to work back from the time that I usually want to get up in the morning, (and in fact according to the number of hours that I feel that I need to sleep) to work out the time I ought to go to bed. I think that most people tend rather to work the other way. My theory about it is that if you have your pattern for getting up and you try to stick more or less to this pattern, whatever is happening in the day, then you have tremendous advantage. You have almost got the day beaten before you start. This is something worth thinking about. I certainly cannot lay down whether you need five or ten or twelve hours a day.

Q In what sort of ways can prayer be a hard grind?

In most ways! Just fitting it in to start with, in finding a time and being sure you are being regular about it. You know how it is; prayer time is the first thing to go. You just have not got time for it. When I say time, I mean you have to give some time to it, not just two minutes; it should be five minutes, ten minutes, a quarter of an hour or something like this. If you have a busy life and you have all sorts of other things to do, you must carve a bit out specially for it, not just a scrap when you are so tired that nothing goes anyhow. To carve a bit out and to stay there with nothing happening, this can in itself be quite a grind. Later on, you can get to a state when the whole of you just rebels against it. It is all so tight and difficult that you just want to get up and run away. It is not that you have not got time; it is just that the whole thing seems to become quite repulsive to you, you almost want to scream perhaps. There are all sorts of things like this. You can very definitely get involved in the nonsense of the whole thing, the non-existence of God, the futility of carrying on like this when you might be doing something else.

Q How useful do you think long repetitive prayers are?

It is important, I would have thought, to begin by realising that all the things that have come into the life of the church apart from the Eucharist, which is the centre of our prayer life and is the only thing essential to it, are simply devotions. They are aids introduced at certain stages to help you as a person to come closer to God and to help you develop your relationship with God. So, talking to you as a medical student (that is to the person asking the question) there have been various times when different things have been tried out for various ailments. And if you have got somebody who cannot walk very well you may try putting their legs in plaster but then this may go out of fashion. Then you decide the only thing to have is deep ray treatment or something like this and then the next you may go on to is having nice hot baths. You keep on trying different things.

As far as we are concerned, something like the rosary did not come into prominence until Saint Dominic, and people got on well before that as far as I know, and I do not think they failed to make contact with God. Then other things like the Stations of the Cross and suchlike grew up, all as aids to devotion. They have come and they have gone. The very famous one they used in England at the time of the Reformation, the Jesus Psalter, is never used at all nowadays. I tried it once at an all-night vigil and was never allowed to do it again! It was very funny, it sent everybody to sleep.

Then take the 'Jesus prayer', used by the Orthodox Church (where one normally prays over and over again the words 'Lord Jesus Christ, have mercy on me a sinner', or similar). This may not necessarily commend itself to all of us in the West, though it may do to some.

But the thing I would think about it is that you

have here something rather like 'music while you work' which keeps a certain rhythm going for you at a certain level though you do not need to concentrate very much on the actual words because they are so repetitive. It does, therefore, if you take it in this way, leave your mind free for some form of meditation if you want it. Personally the only way I use the rosary is to have it in my pocket, and if I am walking anywhere I have my hand in my pocket, and it makes a good kind of repetitive background as I am going along. Then it does not matter, as far as I can see, if I meet Tom, Dick or Harry in the street. It all comes in muddled up with 'Hail Marys' and things, and that is excellent.

But I do not find it personally very helpful to concentrate first on a 'Hail Mary', then a mystery of the rosary, and then a 'Glory be to the Father'. I do not think I ever say a proper rosary but I just go on and on with whatever may come. Sometimes in Lourdes I get into saying the rosary properly because I am saying it with somebody else, with the sick for example. For many people of the younger age group I would think probably it would be useless rather than useful. They may be missing out on something that has been and still is useful to many —but it does not seem to be helpful to everybody today. I do not think you should try and use something that is useless to you, but it can be tried if you have never tried it.

Petition and Intercession

I want to start by trying to say a little about what is called petition and intercession, and to give my definition of these two types of prayer. Petition seems to me to be praying for something, whilst intercession is praying for somebody, and this is the distinction I am going to make here. It is, I believe, quite important to have this distinction. Possibly the term petition is used more in the Church of Rome and allied circles, whereas intercession is probably employed more in other churches such as the Church of England.

It appears that petition in the sense of praying for something presents a real problem for people today. I suppose, in our rather practical way of thinking, we have come to the conclusion, that what with weather satellites and various things of this nature, it is not sensible to imagine that we can pray for a change in the weather! However, I have my doubts whether that is true, for the most extraordinary things do seem to happen! As far as I can see our weather is very unpredictable, even with satellites! If you look at the scriptures there seems no doubt at all that it was common practice in the Old Testament days to pray for things to happen. I suppose it is possible for us to cut this out completely and say, well, we accept the ideas of the Old Testament and the history of the people of God, but, of course, they were very primitive and nowadays we understand we cannot pray for this sort of thing to happen.

But look at Christ! You find Christ saying the most extravagant things, things which we frankly just don't believe. If you have a modicum of faith and you say to this mountain, be removed and cast yourself into the sea, it will do so. Well, I think I have a little faith, but I have never managed to move that sort of mountain, other mountains perhaps, but that sort I have never removed personally. Yet he does say: "Go on asking, ask and you shall receive, seek and you shall find, knock and it shall be opened." He gives the instance of the importunate person who comes in the middle of the night and bangs on the house door, and the man of the house says: "I am in bed and my children are in bed, go away." But because the caller goes on banging, the man eventually gets up and gives him some bread. Again on another occasion Christ says: "Does a father give a child a stone when the child asks for bread?" I just want to suggest that we may be doing less than justice to God if we completely eliminate the possibility of praying for things to happen, because, though theoretically we know a certain amount about what is going to happen, I repeat it is, in my opinion, quite extraordinary what odd things can and do happen. I just want to open your minds to this. Ponder on it, because I think that in this age praying for anything in particular can too easily be dismissed as pointless.

Well, why should I think that there might be a point to it? It seems to me that asking, petitioning, answers a very basic need in human beings. Humanly we spend a tremendous amount of time asking things of people. We ask of each other practically all the time. You did not actually ask me to write about prayer; but I have done. So your reading is tantamount to your asking to be told something about prayer. You are asking "teach me to pray" just as Christ was asked by the apostles.

When you think of it, every time a woman walks into a room she is really, if she is anything of a woman, asking to be admired by all the men there. That is why she walks in a particular sort of way and does her hair in a particular fashion. She is asking to be accepted and acknowledged and so on. When we speak, we are asking to be listened to. There are so many different ways in which we ask during our daily life. We ask for things as well as asking for a development in relationship. I will come to this later.

It opens in us, humanly speaking, the gates of charity because when somebody asks us for something, then we either respond or don't respond in giving this thing. We are often asked for things which, for one reason or another, we do not think we should go on with and accede to. Sometimes too, we are asked for things that we just cannot do. We cannot do it, because we have not got the power to do it. It appears to me—and this may be just an anthropomorphic projection—that it is probable that we will have something of this kind of relationship with God in our petition and our petitionary prayer, because it seems so very fundamental to our human nature. And I would not like you to feel that this is a waste of time.

Of course it comes in scripture that God knows what we want, and so we are told not to pray with a great deal of language to God who knows our every desire and hears us when we pray to him in secret. Nevertheless, this implies too that there must be some sort of opening to God in which we say please: "Please this, please that, please the other." And therefore all I want to say at this stage with regard to petitionary prayer is that first and foremost it seems to be basic to our human nature to ask, of a parent, or a teacher, of a guide, of somebody who has greater knowledge than we have, of a friend, of almost everybody. Therefore I would think that it follows that it is basic that we should ask of God.

But within this asking, there are all sorts of different things we ought to be thinking about. First of all, we want to be humble about what we ask for. When a child asks, it tends not to be able to use its mind very much, it simply says: "I want, give me" and this sort of thing. And as far as this is concerned, we adopt the same sort of attitude. At a later stage, particularly perhaps with regard to the relationship with another person, we may be able in humility to introduce into that relationship of asking some clause like 'if you don't mind' or 'if this is convenient' or something of this sort. 'If you really don't want it, then I'd like it.' There must be some sort of humility basic to it.

Then I think we need to have a real openness about this which is connected, of course, with the question of trying to find God's will. What do we instance? Clearly the sort of thing we are tied up in. We may desperately want to get this particular job, or we may very much want to pass this examination, or pass the driving test, or whatever it may be. We want that. We may pray about it. Now is this, in fact, totally irrelevant to our passing the driving test, examination, or whatever? It may be.

Here, though it may seem totally absurd to us today, I want you to consider the possibility of the economy of God, which is the basis of the whole thing, somehow or other working into our relationship with him. I do not think one can pin-point this, and it is something that can seem very unreasonable to a lot of people. Nevertheless, so many peculiar things have happened in my own life that it does seem to me possible that things can happen.

I think we have got to be much more open than we are normally to the possibility of things happening. I am sure there is some explanation for the story which I am going to tell. I remember extremely well when I was six or seven and my brother was a couple of years older than me, that he was very bored on a very brilliantly fine afternoon in the summer— I can't think why we were bored that particular day. At any rate he said that the only thing he wanted was a thunderstorm, and so he started to pray for a thunderstorm, and quite suddenly there was a terrific clap of thunder. I don't suppose it made him very much better at prayer. However, you have to be prepared for things to happen if you are ready to live in relationship with God, though it may sound completely nonsensical. I am quite clear about this.

But on the other hand, whereas one has to have

the simplicity of the dove, one also has to have in a certain sense the wisdom of the serpent. For it is quite clear, and we must make it quite clear, that you cannot neglect your work for an examination, and then go on to say: "But I do go to Mass every day, therefore I will get a good degree." It just does not work that way, so we cannot expect (that is where humility comes in and the seeking of God's will) that these things will necessarily happen. There is a sense in which it is heads he wins, and tails I lose really, because if the prayer I make is answered, we say how wonderful God is, and if it is not answered we say, well then we must realise that God's will may not be this. So he wins both ways! We have to see this as being a difficulty which we can only find the way through by constant living by faith.

Therefore, one always ends up with the prayer of Christ in the garden: "Not my will but thine be done", "if this can pass from me . . ." Also of course, it is true, in asking for a particular thing, one is probably asking for something one has not any real idea about; it seems for oneself that this particular thing will be something that ought to be done by God because. . . . And quite often looking back at a later stage one sees in fact the whole sense of God's purpose. I have an old friend who says quite solemnly when something happens: "Well, I think God was quite right about that." Sometimes one catches up with God in this, as it were, and sees that whereas we would have arranged it in this particular way, he in fact has arranged it in a completely different way. So be open about this.

We must be clear that asking gets us into the right kind of attitude to God. Asking means that we do not regard ourselves as self-sufficient like the

Pharisee, and indicates a degree of humility rather like the publican. We cannot come close to God if we think we are self-sufficient. To ask for virtues, holiness and so on can be much less humble and genuine than a cry from the heart for some immediate, actual, temporal need. We should ask for what we want and not for what we think we should want. And if we can grow in openness to God, he can lead us to the point when we come to pray for what he would like for us—God does not impose things on us, but he wants us to want them. It may be that that's God's first move to get us to want something.

Then finally this question of perseverance. I can have a very deep conviction myself about something though I do not know the time or date as it were, and I can say to God, "Well, I think you are being pretty stupid about this thing and personally I think it should be done this way". I think you have every right to go on like this saying, "But after all then you may be wiser than I am, so perhaps you are not as stupid as I think you are"— that sort of sense of praying. God does want you to go on persevering in prayer. He wants you to go on, because in this way you may grow to understand his ways better.

You could liken it to someone sailing or cooking, or somebody doing a garden or somebody doing almost anything. If you are not particularly expert you tend to say "surely you ought to take that pot off before it burns" and the person cooking it simply does not pay any attention at all, and you can go on saying this, and, at the moment when you think it is too late, they take it off and in fact it is done perfectly. But you would have taken it off earlier! Or if you are an expert at sailing and you are tacking into the wind or whatever it may be, the actual moment at which you tack the other way is a very nice point. If you are not an expert, as I am not, the probability is that you do not hang on long enough. You have as it were to accept the fact that God wants you to hang on that little bit longer. It is often God's way with us to keep us waiting for something until it seems too late, and then to give us what we want, so we have to have the courage to learn to hang on until that moment comes.

Well, now let us look at intercession, which is asking something for somebody. All the things I have said so far are also true of intercession for other people. But in addition to this I think we have got to see much more clearly that with another person we are not at all able to understand at what point the suffering, the trial, the tension, and so on is going to become unbearable or whatever it may be, because we are not really ourselves quite *au fait* with how that person's character should be developed. I think behind all we are doing and thinking, must be the sense that God really is willing the development, the salvation and fullness of individual A and individual B for whom we are saying to God: "please let this happen to this person", "please let that happen". And God is far more aware of what is necessary for this person than we are, which takes it largely out of our own hands.

But basic here again is the whole question of how God's economy actually works with regard to people and to things, and this is something that we shall never fully understand this side of heaven. May it not be that the working out (surely where brother helps brother and so on) of the whole of this life we are in, not only depends on the redemptive work of Christ, but also depends on the co-operation that you and I are putting into it in our own lives? So

I do not know, as I write, what effect this is going to have on your life. On one hand it may drive you to say: "Well that is the end of that, it's obviously no more prayer for me, the whole thing is too childish." Another person may go off and become a hermit and devote the whole of his life to prayer because of this book. For the vast majority, it will be forgotten in a few weeks' time. This is the way things go.

I just don't know, but I have to believe that what I am trying to do is working into the pattern of the development of life where I am and, insofar as it has repercussions, in the world as from now. I believe that God in his economy, his plan of salvation, knows that I am here and is fool enough to entrust me with this particular message at this particular time, and is fool enough to allow you the openness to say, this is ridiculous, or this is alright. And that it is alright may be equally foolish as that it is ridiculous. This is what we are up against. And for this reason, therefore, I think when you get into a puzzle about this, you have to go right back into the whole redemptive plan of God. The basic Christian position on this is that you and I are co-operating in the plan of redemption; we co-operate insofar as God himself is concerned but also co-operate insofar as the world is concerned, whether it is by giving a cup of cold water to somebody or whether it is by praying for somebody.

Again if you want to come down to specific details I think the whole thing can become almost extraordinarily absurd. One of the stories that I use as an illustration of this is an occasion when I was a student of theology in Rome. It was a very hot sultry sirocco day and in the morning we had a lecture on the sacrament of penance; it was very hot in the lecture room, the sun beating down on the tin roof, and I was in a terribly bolshy mind about the whole thing and very sleepy. The lecturer started off by saying: "In the twentieth chapter of Saint John you find the statement of Christ which is the basis of the sacrament of penance, 'whose sins you forgive, they are forgiven'." I thought, "Right. I know that," and I went to sleep. When I woke up he was saying: "John 20, whose sins you forgive, they are forgiven," so I went to sleep again. I woke up and heard "if you want to prove . . . John 20". I was absolutely tearing my hair and fed up with the whole thing.

In the afternoon I had to go a long hot walk to see somebody in hospital the other end of Rome, and there I was in my flat hat and long skirt-like soutane and not able to afford to go by bus because I was a poor student. I was thoroughly fed up, wondering if I had a vocation, whether God existed, why it was so hot, how sweaty I was, the whole thing was absolute hell! I came past the church of Saint John Lateran, and there was no one about, for everyone was sensibly having a siesta. Then I came into the little cobbled street near Saint John Lateran and there was a young man sweeping the road, which was a very odd thing to be doing at that time of day. As I came past he leaned on his broom and said in his best Italian, could he speak to me, and I said in my worst Italian that I was not Italian, so he said "Good". Then he said could I tell him something because he was living with communists in his lodgings and they were arguing about scripture and they said to him that there was no place in scripture where it said anything about the sacrament of penance and could I tell him if this was so! Now I was carrying a little New Testament with me so I brought it out to show him it was in the twentieth chapter of Saint John, and he, of course, was absolutely delighted!

When this sort of thing begins to happen one begins to wonder! So there are coincidences and very strange things occur, and it seems to me that we fail to see this dimension in the life that we live. I think it is tremendously important that we should be more aware of the impact that we may have on other people, just by word, or by anything.

Also on the question of intercession I want to say one or two things more. First of all it is very important for us to be, as it were, alongside people; just to be there and let them feel and know of our support. I like the idea that when Peter was in prison, the whole church of God at that time got together to pray for him. I am sure he had a sense of this although he did not know what would happen. In fact he probably did not think anything would. But when the angel came, perhaps then he may have had a sense of the church of God praying for him. I think there can be a tremendous moral support, or whatever you like to call it, when we are praying for each other, interceding for each other. I would certainly feel this on a psychological level apart from anything spiritual. I am sure this is why it is very necessary for us to try to come together in prayer at the Eucharist and in prayer groups.

It is also very important for us to know other people are praying for us. This I would think is one of the reasons behind such a thing as the working of the enclosed contemplative communities. It is important for us to have a real sense of the possibility of supporting other people because we are alongside them. Now this is not simply praying in the sense of getting down on one's knees and saying "Lord help so and so because they are in distress". We ourselves have to be involved in the difficulties of the world. If you take the state of the world at this particular moment, what sort of problems are there? Well, obviously there are problems of faith.

Anyone, I think, who is in any way praying and united to God will, almost inevitably, be involved in problems of faith, because it is part of the working out of salvation in the world at the moment that we should have these problems of faith. Therefore we would not be part of the incarnate church, the living Body of Christ, if we were not involved in these. We have got to be alongside humanity in a willing sort of way. We have not got all the time to be saying, "For heaven's sake God, take this away, make my faith sure because otherwise I'll give up". We have got to say, "Lord go on with this if you want to, if in the problems and troubles I am having myself and am enduring in faith, I can in fact help your suffering Body which is the church". And so on through morals, through the liturgy, through everything.

We are not meant necessarily to be sailing along easily, but we are meant to be taking up the cross alongside people. Your suffering goes much further than simply saying "Pray for me. I have a pain in the neck". It is really that we are meant to be involved in the very suffering of mankind. If you take this as being so, then the intercessory power of the church's prayer must cover all strata of society and all possible eventualities in life. We must have in prayer the mentally deficient as part of the world as we know it. We must have spastics, as they are part of the world as we know it. We must have the rich and the poor, we must have the people who are having doubts, we must have the people who are involved in all the difficulties of sexual relationship and other things. Unless we are involved in every single way and somehow living for Christ within this, we do not have the power to cover the plurality of God in the world, the plurality of mankind in the world. Therefore our particular cross, our particular penitential nature that we are involved in, has its own part to play in the intercession for the whole world.

It may be, and I find it does happen with people, that one can say: "Well here you are, you can offer your life in this way for the people like this, because you have the advantage of having faith; you have the power to pray, the will to offer yourself." There is one particular woman who comes to Lourdes every year from Ireland, while I am working there. She has to be flat on her back the whole time and in addition to that she is completely deaf and cannot hear a single thing, and so she has to write everything she wants to convey. Also she is in fairly continual pain and she cannot even sit up. She writes to me often all the year round. She lives in a Cheshire Home in Ireland and she says people often say what is the use. It seems to me that it is of enormous use, because there are lots of people in Cheshire Homes and there are lots of people who are suffering in this way and have nothing behind them at all, they have no sense of God or what suffering can mean. It would seem to me that a person like her who would accept this sort of possibility of intercession has got an enormous amount that she can do for other people, though perhaps they won't ever understand it—not this side of heaven.

Then finally in this form of intercession, as in

petition, one must as far as possible be aligned to the will of God. We just don't know. It will be fascinating to find out when we get to heaven eventually why such and such a thing happened. In the meantime it is very important, always if we possibly can, (though it is very difficult sometimes to get to the bottom of our prayer, to the very foundation of it) to remember the fact that God himself knows very much better than we do what it is that is necessary for a particular person.

Going right back, a considerable number of years now, I knew a boy who was fifteen or sixteen years old when he died. He had lost a leg with cancer, and his mother had died of cancer, his father had left his mother and the other children were in an orphanage, and people would say to me when I was trying to help him through when he was dying of cancer: "I suppose you are praying that he will get better", or "I hope that you will have a cure", or "Couldn't you take him to Lourdes". I had a rather, perhaps wrong, fatalistic attitude because I was saying to God: "Well right, if you want him to get well, do, but it seems to me you would do far better to have him in heaven because people are not terribly kind to those who have only one leg—it would be nice if they were kinder—but he has no background, no family, not very much education." I was very open about the whole situation, because it seemed to me it would be very wise if he took the boy to heaven quickly. And in fact he did take him to heaven about fourteen or fifteen years ago; if he was alive now, he would be something over thirty. I don't know! It might have been awfully good for him, and God obviously could have worked the whole thing out in another way. But I think God was very wise to take him when he did. Personally, though I was very sad to see him go, I was very happy also in a sense that he did go in that way. So we must be open, as I see it, about this question of the outcome of our interceding.

Q Why should God make us wait so long for our prayers to be answered?

It depends, of course, on how we wait. If we wait in irritation, it can turn us away from God and embitter us which is very difficult for us to understand. But when you find a person who is prepared to wait in a constructive sort of way, we get right to the heart of God and we are reminded of Paul who, talking about charity starts off by saying "charity is patient". God takes an awfully long time; think of all the ages which we have had since the beginning of the world and we don't seem to have got really very far, or all the time we have had since the Incarnation. Each of us only has a certain span.

It rather implies also that we expect to get to a certain point by a certain time, but we don't know what point God is expecting us to get to. We want, perhaps, to be much more cut and dried than he does. I would have thought it is enormously important for us to accept something of the long term planning of God. This is especially important with regard to people messing up their lives with sin and what have you. A particular down period seen over a life span may be absolutely vital to the coming back. The sort of thing about which here and now one says: "Oh goodness, he is making a mess of his life" may be the only thing that is going to straighten him out. God presumably has patience and vision to see the whole thing through, but it is very difficult for us.

Q How do you answer the question that prayer is deluding self?

Well, you have to begin on faith and try to get yourself straight on the existence of God. If there is a God existent, and you can believe this, the likelihood of contact with him seems to be fairly fundamental. If you don't, then I suppose you just go round talking to yourself. I don't see why you shouldn't. So really it all depends on faith. Then, of course, beyond faith, in actual practical instruction if you were reading the gospels and you thought what this man said was a good thing, then you would have to try in some way to follow what he had said.

Q Isn't it rather a vicious circle, if you pray to get faith and yet can't pray unless you have faith?

I do not think this follows somehow. You can't start to pray if you have not got faith, yet you say you are praying to have faith, so perhaps the faith has already been anticipated. Saint Paul in Romans 10:9, writes that you can only say 'Jesus is Lord' by the power of the Holy Spirit. So probably you can only talk to me if you go back as far as this; if you believe in God, you believe that, if you don't you just accept that it is a natural human process or evolutionary process. It is breaking out of a circle.

Q Should we not pray for things more important than the weather?

I am not advocating that you simply start off by praying about the weather! My point in giving this as an illustration is that I do not know if man has solved the weather question. I think the present tendency is to think that this is all very childish, as you do. I have tried simply to right the balance.

Obviously the sort of thing you ought to be praying about eventually is that the will of God be done. Now humanly speaking, I am not certain that you can get people to start this way. I am only saying that as human beings very naturally we tend to ask for what we want. As far as I can see in the gospels Christ advocates that we ask for what we want. If you are adult, you ought to be asking for things other than a child would ask for, and this depends on your own growth. And if you grow in Christ then it seems to me you get a combination; you pray desperately for something or for somebody and yet at the same time you have this tremendously relaxed approach—almost leaving it to God. I find it difficult to put into words.

It means that you have to put your whole heart and soul into being with somebody in a prayer or asking for something, and yet at the same time to have complete confidence that God's will is what really matters. But if I may say so, I think this is some way on. It is very negative to say to people you ought not to pray for this or for that. I think, for example, an old countrywoman in Ireland, who is telling her beads perhaps for a fine day for the garden fête for the local parish may have at the same time a sense of the will of God. She will say to God: "Glory be to God, it is a nice soft day" (or something like this). And it will all work out in God's will, for though she is absolutely battering away on her beads at it she has a certain sense of leaving it to God.

Now I think the whole thing seems much less sensible when you are much less involved in it. Obviously if you just teach children to get down and say a prayer and that, this done, everything will be all right, you are just instructing them wrongly about the way things work. I take the weather as an example, for obviously there is an explanation for the way the weather goes, but my word, you just look at the weather forecasts! You are told exactly what it is going to do, and wake up the following morning to find it is doing the reverse.

Q What would you say about praying for the dead?

I don't know quite what to say about this. Here again perhaps we are starting from the wrong angle. We as human beings feel a need that we can carry on with people. If we can accept that there is an after life, we must accept that there is some connection between us and the after life. And if we further accept that there are some forms of division in the after life, then one is in the state of relationship still with the person who has died. As we understand it, the person will either be with God in happiness, in which case they should be praying for us with God. So you have the opportunity of saying to them "If you are with God in heaven, then for heaven's sake help me." Or if in God's economy purification (or whatever you would call it) takes place before they are fit to see God, then obviously your prayer is going to have some effect.

All we can say is that this has been the tradition of the church from very early times, from the times of Tertullian onward or, before the time of Christ, if you take the book of Maccabees as being canonical. The essence of the thing was you could not only pray for people while they were still alive but, because of the communion of saints, you would continue to pray for them after death and this would be effective. Death is, after all, a change and not a break. So much of this is based on God's economy which you probably don't understand any more than the economists do ours! You do what you can to put the thing right.

It carries on, as it seems to me, from what you were doing in the preceding time here in this world. How does my intercession help? It may help simply psychologically, and it may help you because God's economy works this way. It may help you because it changes someone else's psychology. There are all sorts of different things it may do. If I don't pray for you, is the outcome going to be totally different? Well, I don't know what God's plan is about this. All I know is that I must do what I can to help you. If you come to me and say "Please lend me twenty-five pence", I say "Well, look, there are lots of other people in the world, why not ask them?" But the fact of the matter is that you have come to ask me, and so I am the person at the moment who has to decide if I am going to help you or not. And it isn't an answer to say "God will provide. Go away my dear". At that particular moment I am the person who can save you from a night out or whatever it is. And at another time I am the person who God wants to pray for you; and if you are dead, and I know you and am moved to pray for you, then this is a pretty good sign that this is something God wants me to do to help you.

Surely it is important for us to have a continuation of our own relationship, and therefore you are more likely perhaps to pray for some people than others. The connection here is like the connection between a family being particularly keen to help its own kith and kin. The idea of communion of saints after all is that if you have been particularly interested in the Simon community here, then all the people in the Simon community ought to be praying for you because you have always been their angel of comfort and so they maintain this relationship with you. It may seem rather crude and anthropomorphic, but perhaps it gives a sense of the way the thing works.

Q I don't see how God's saving will can be changed by my requesting that it should be changed. Why should the expression of his love be altered by what I want or ask for?

Why should not the expression of God's love take into account that you are going to be involved in this?

Meditation

In the previous chapters I have been trying to build up a foundation of prayer. Now I want specifically to discuss meditation. Meditation has in some sense come into vogue as it were with the Maharishi and transcendental meditation, but the meditation I am going to discuss will not be particularly transcendental. Meditation is, and has been, in the Western Christian tradition, and, I imagine, beyond Christian bodies, a term which has been used for a long time. And like many terms and ideas, because it has had such a long usage, it has to some extent gone out of favour. Today, perhaps, people feel meditation is something they get hung up over, and they are not terribly keen to think that this is an important part of their prayer life. Indeed, quite a lot of people would want to plunge into a much deeper form of prayer and leave meditation aside, and never try to go through it at all.

So let me first of all give some idea of what meditation is in the sense that I am going to write about it. Meditation for us as individuals, is to take some thought into our minds and to work on it with our minds. And clearly as far as meditation as such is concerned it does not have to be in regard to God. But the specific kind of meditation that I am discussing, has to be at least in regard to God, the Kingdom of God, the purpose of man in this universe and things of this sort. It has, therefore, an enormously wide range. You can think about all kinds of subjects that are in the realm of philosophy, for example goodness, truth, beauty. For a Christian they will have some relationship to God, to the Ultimate. We can meditate more specifically in terms of the revelation of God when we come down to Biblical meditation where we may take a part of a Psalm, of the Old Testament, or of the New Testament and study this in greater depth with the use of the mind.

There is a very close connection here between what meditation is and what is actual study in the way of scripture or theology. It is sometimes said that it is all right to meditate during your theology, but you must not theologise during your meditation. The idea being, I presume, that if one is not careful when one is meditating one gets into something that is much too systematic and too intellectualised to be what meditation is really getting at. Meditation should help us to greater understanding of God, his creation, his purpose, our relationship to that purpose, in terms of fulfilling ourselves and in terms of coming to love him more. Abbot Chapman in talking about meditation said the object of meditating is to arrive at loving, whereas I suppose theology as such is more directed just at knowing things, and working them out intellectually, than at loving.

Well, one of the problems about meditation in a

way is that it has in the western church and particularly in the Roman Catholic Church, been given almost a bad name by some people because it has often been made into such a rigid sort of system. It rather parallels the problems that we are having now over the structure of the church where people feel that the structure seems to get in the way of what the church is about. But the invention, and the systematisation of meditation was simply something that was developed in order to try and help people to construct a way in which they could pursue their ideas, develop their ideas, ponder on them and so on. And it was not originally, as far as I can see, particularly formal; people thought about what Christ had said, and then from there went on to preaching what Christ had said. At a later stage when the scriptures were more available they thought about them and this of course was meditation.

Saint Benedict, for example, who precedes the ordinary formal Catholic type of meditation had no formal meditation in his Rule. For him the rhythm of life was in community and was threefold. The first part of the rhythm was the Divine office which was said in community. It was partly made up of psalms recited vocally, and besides forming the basis of the community praise, was a source of private cogitation for the monks. The psalms while expressing the minds of their authors came to reflect and affect the minds of the monks who recited them. Within the office also were scripture readings which again formed part of the something that they could imbibe mentally. The office was to be virtually a prolonged contemplation as suggested in Psalm 118 (119), "How I love thy law, O God, all day long I think on it". They also had the Mass, the Eucharist, which was part of the first phase of their life. Then secondly, they had extended periods of *lectio divina*, that is of spiritual reading, in which they read something on their own, probably the scriptures or the fathers' explanations of the scriptures. These they read and pondered on in a meditative sort of way. Then thirdly, there was manual labour which formed for them a useful kind of worry bead. For the monks were able, whilst getting on with ordinary daily tasks when their minds were to some extent fairly free, to ruminate on the ideas they had received from the Divine office with its reading of the scriptures and from the Mass, as well as on the thoughts they had picked up from their spiritual reading. There was not anything particularly systematised about this. As far as I know, they were not told to sit down and think in a particular way.

Meditation became more systematised with the coming into being of the more active orders and with lay people becoming involved with it. On the whole the Benedictine order had little to do with this development. And it came to be felt as things went on, I suppose particularly with people like Saint Ignatius, that the mind needed a system to work on, and in the later fifteenth and sixteenth centuries this system of meditation became more formalised. The question-mark nowadays is whether at this stage in your own development (and this is where it becomes quite personal to you) you find it useful to have such a system. And if you do find it useful then you should by all means use it and develop it for yourselves, not feeling that you must do it exactly as it is set down in a book, though there are many books on meditation mainly produced by Jesuits, because this became very much their approach.

What do I mean by systematise? Well, bearing

in mind still that the object is to arrive at loving, what meditation is largely involved in doing is to give people a better understanding, mentally and intellectually speaking, of the person and situation about which they are meditating in order to inform them so that they can then be able to carry a sense of this person through life with them. When I say this person, of course I am talking about Christ. But in order to do this the general idea, again as I understand it, is that you need to use all the faculties which can be such a worry to people, that is you need to take up your imagination, to have your mind working as well, and also if you possibly can, to get yourself enthused in this so that your heart is involved in it too. Perhaps all these distinctions (imagination, mind, heart) are just scholastic, but the object was to involve the whole person in meditation. Of course in past days they did not have marvellous visual aids such as the TV, film strips and things of this sort, though in fact I don't know that many people do use these for meditation, but nevertheless they are there.

The general idea was that you started off your meditation by setting the scene for the situation whatever it might be. The setting of his scene was something from scripture and was really very simple because you tried to imagine yourself back into whatever the situation might be. In Lent the subject might be Christ in the desert, and so perhaps you might read a historical geography or something like this which would give a description of what the desert was like so that you could picture it for yourself. Then you set yourself alongside Christ in this position, and from there you progressed to the essential part of your meditation which might be, for example, on penance or on sin, or the need for some form of mortification, or on Christ himself in this situation, or on the possibility of temptation within such a situation, and so on. This depends very much on the particular story which you have chosen. From there you move on to refer this back to yourself. Having perhaps seen how Christ responds in the desert to the temptations of the devil, you then say yes, but now I am there and I am faced with the temptation, what is the situation with regard to myself in the terms of Christ's response? Then you move on, perhaps, to make as a final conclusion to your meditation some resolution about the way you yourself should try to face up to whatever trials you are having in life at this particular moment.

So it has been quite a practical development. It is also meant to help develop some understanding of Christ and yourself. You see him, you feel him, you realise him in this situation and you should, therefore, be somehow drawn towards him, come to know him better, come to know him in depth, and this should somehow move your heart, inspire you to love for him, to desire to imitate him, to be with him in his suffering whatever it may be. And the meditation, therefore, is meant to go from the simply imaginative and the intellectual into something which is going really to rouse you to co-operation with Christ, to live with Christ and eventually to the love of Christ, and on and on.

Now one of the things that can happen with meditation, of course, is that people find it awfully difficult if they are trying to make a new resolution every day, because, for example, by the end of Lent you will have got no less than forty resolutions which you are going to carry out, and to keep the whole thing going is like juggling. People have also found it difficult in meditation to arrive each time at some form of conclusion. The conclusion was sometimes known as a 'spiritual bouquet' which is the name that the French following this approach give it. The use of formal meditation has also meant that people have often tended to be left as it were in their own mental development and not to have stretched beyond this into something very much deeper in the knowledge of God. I am not saying that this always happens but it is something that can happen, and I think that there is a danger here.

Now we could say as a general rule that most people are capable of thinking, and thinking about, and therefore most people are capable of this sort of exercise, thinking about God. It can be very closely aligned to theology; it can be something which comes from spiritual reading and it is something which each one of us who is interested in God, in Christianity and so on is practically bound to do in some sort of way. The question mark is on whether or not this is a valid way of praying as opposed to something that comes into your life in the ordinary course of events. What I mean by that is, am I justified in saying I am going into church to spend five mintes, ten minutes, half an hour, whatever it may be, with God; and being there in church with him, take the Bible, take a passage from it, set the scene, etc. and go through the sort of process that I have been suggesting to you? For several centuries now this has been the common way in which people have been taught, particularly in seminaries and religious communities in order to develop their relationship with God.

But though this has been a common way of teaching people and though it has a great deal to be said for it in certain stages, the difficulty here for most people is that the practice becomes more and more difficult because the first joy and enthusiasm of tackling it this way and the obvious good that comes out of it, tend to fade and the mind gets bogged down and blocked. You cannot get the thoughts that you used to have; you no longer find yourself moved in any way by the example of Christ and you begin to think: "Well, Good Lord, I am just wasting my time here; somehow I must have gone wrong!" And people have, I think, largely struggled with this and spent many months and years, sometimes in tremendous dryness, trying to tackle this form of meditating. And sometimes this has led to their abandoning the whole thing, and at other times it has given way to a grim determination to stay in church and simply spend the period fighting the numerous distractions that come when a person finds this particular form of praying difficult and unrewarding.

In the next chapter, I am going to suggest that at a certain stage I believe that it is necessary for everybody to be completely brave and to realise that this excellent method is not the one that is suitable at the stage I have just described. You must go forward into something that is far less organised and you will find that the period of time you spend with God will be occupied in a different sort of way. This does not mean that you abandon altogether your thinking about God, for you will continue to have a very real need to develop your understanding of God, and spiritual reading, the *lectio divina*, of the monks becomes the source of your prayer in a deeper way. And so instead of going into your room, into a church, into a chapel or wherever it may be to spend time with God to use this as a meditative period, the meditative period now occurs when you are actually reading. You may be reading a book about the scriptures, reading the scriptures themselves, reading a book about virtue, about anything, the constitutions of Vatican II; a hundred and one things are possible. As you go on also the field for meditation becomes wider and wider and wider, because there are so many things that are immensely interesting and spark off thoughts.

For example in a Russian novel, *The First Circle,* which I recently read, I have come across two things that I find very interesting. One was something to the effect that if you go on living your whole life looking over your shoulder, you cannot remain human. Now that is a tremendous thing to think about because so many of us spend a lot of our time looking over our shoulders, whether it is in the church looking at bishops, or in ordinary life looking at police or whatever it may be. This is something, it seems to me, you may well take up as meditation; it comes out of a novel, it comes out of Russia, should this not be a tremendous reason to use it to meditate on? Again in this novel something is said to the effect that the greatest invention of a brilliant person seems rather insignificant to a greater mind. This puts everybody into their rightful place. Things like this which you can come across in this sort of way can prove fruitful, quite apart from things you read in the newspaper and other things like that. It is important to see the way in which everything can move towards this approach.

Now I would like to mention at this point that there are various ways in the particular age in which we are living for this meditation to take place. First of all there is the individual meditation which I have discussed where you or I take something up and read it and think about it. There is also the possibility of just listening to sermons, of the sort of community reaction you get to the readings in the Eucharist, and things of this sort. At the present time as we are in a way more community-minded, I think there is a very real need for us to see the importance of the group meditation. As a result of a group coming together to read the scriptures and by bringing their own particular mentality together there is the possibility of complementing each other and sparking off thoughts from each other which are certainly communal. This has a very real validity and should help when you come by yourself to be alone with God for you will have new trains of thought to draw on and to develop. We can help each other enormously in this way. So I think the group meeting as such is something that we ought to regard as being useful, and still with us.

A side issue of this, perhaps, is the question of what happens with married couples and their praying together. For obvious reasons I am not expert in this but all I can say from my knowledge of married couples praying is that it is not an easy problem to tackle. But one of the ways I would have thought very useful is to read the scriptures or something else together and to make this exchange a way of getting into each other's mind and heart on the situation which you are studying. And it may be that this will lead into your being quiet together in a meditative kind of way in which the only thing you have is this physical union of being together, as at this point you will have to lapse into your own communion with God. This is just something I throw out as a possibility.

I don't think there is much else I want to say about meditation, but to re-emphasise that the ordinary way where you start on vocal prayer, move on to meditation and then on beyond meditation into something else, is something that is still valid. It is, however, by no means an absolute and universal approach. If, therefore, in your own approach to prayer you have found that you have managed to plunge straight into a much more open form of prayer in which meditation is not really present at all and you are just with God and in the sort of development that I am going to discuss in the next chapter, that is excellent. Do not feel: "I have gone wrong somewhere, I have not meditated, I must go back and do it"; rather think in terms of developing through your spiritual reading. I am sure we would all accept that we are not just trying to be illuminated in what we are doing, but we are trying to learn of God in any human way that we have, so the use of our mind on the things of God is something that is very important. I believe that this use of the mind will continue in one way or another, during the whole course of our lives.

I would like to end by simply saying that when we are just with God in prayer time, we do not perhaps need to have wonderful thoughts about God then for we are in fact with him. However when we are moving about, going from one place to another, when it is difficult for us to get into what I would call a very deep sense of communion with God, it can be very useful indeed to have something to get our minds working on which is in relation to him. Therefore teasing out a problem about God as you are walking from one place to another, can be very useful indeed as a way of bringing yourself to a position so that when you are actually with him, you can be more open and much less on your intellectual level but beyond it as it were. This is something which I think is very important. Therefore as with vocal prayer, which as I have said is something that will last your lifetime, so in this way too the meditative aspect of your prayer will also last a lifetime.

Q What definition of prayer links it up with meditation?

The old definition of prayer which we used to have in the penny catechism was that 'prayer was the raising of the mind and heart to God'. So that when you are specifically thinking about God, this would class as raising of your mind to God. When the heart does not actually get moved in meditation then I think meditation is in danger of becoming simply a theological exercise, and therefore it does not come into this strict definition of prayer. Whereas if you are studying something in the hope of rising towards God, this would come within the definition of prayer. If you take prayer at a much wider level then almost anything you do would come into prayer.

Q Do you not think the study of theology can help you to pray?

I am not wanting to oust theology and if you are actually meditating on it, this is excellent. I am not a theologian, but I think there is a danger if theology becomes too much of an intellectual exercise, it may not raise the heart to God at all. What you are trying to do is to tease out how it is that the church explains the three Persons in one God or something like this, and it is the formulation of this into an intellectual or philosophical type of concept that is really the object of what you are trying to do. Whether or not it moves you to think 'Gosh, isn't God marvellous' may not come into it.

Q Do you not think that theology can be concerned with better knowledge and better love of God?

It would be nice if it always was! We would

have to ask a theologian what he starts studying theology for. It could be that you start studying theology because you want to love God more, but it may be because you have decided that you want to teach theology.

It isn't a question of rules, it is just the question of what the primary aim is. I am afraid that there are a number of theologians who know a great deal about God but do not seem to know him very well. This is the difficulty! I sometimes feel, rightly or wrongly, if you consider another subject such as English, that you can get a certain number of people who can dissect Shakespeare but do not seem to have an enormous lot of time for him. Perhaps this is just my ignorance.

Q Doesn't doing things with others in joy, pleasure and so on constitute part of one's whole prayer to God?

The idea of everything being in some way connected with God and part, therefore, of your prayer depends on the point of origin as far as you are concerned. I do not think that if you are sharing the joy of a rugger match with someone who has no belief in God at all, that this links both of you with God, though you may feel a tremendous enthusiasm for human nature and God's expression of virility in this regard. But this would be very subjective and I don't think you can just take somebody to a rugger field and say: "Here is a meditation on God." But from your point of view this might be something which at the end of the match made you say: "O God, isn't it marvellous to be a man?" I think it must depend to some extent on the point of origin, mustn't it?

Q But can't you talk to your friend who doesn't believe in God and relate it to God in a certain sense?

Well, he can say: "I think you are mad!" In exactly the same way, presented with a page with some figures on it, a mathematician may say "Oh" in enthusiasm and you say "what on earth are you getting excited about?" and he could say "Oh, look at it", because he is a mathematician. To me it is just a few figures on a bit of paper, but to him it is a new revelation! I just have not got the language or the message. It seems to me that this is possible, but he can communicate enthusiasm to me over this. Ideally speaking, we could maintain God ought to be somehow available to every individual and that the enthusiasm can be caught by other individuals in some way or other. But it does not seem that of necessity because I have got it somebody else will catch it, though it can work this way.

Q It can happen surely that we can divorce our experience and experience in the world from other people and then not relate it enough to God?

Yes. I would agree with that completely and this is why the point of origin counts. If you yourself are living in the presence of God, then everything will relate to it. This was what I was trying to get at about reading a novel like *The First Circle*. You can pick things out of it for meditation if you happen to be like that, though other people may say: "Well this is ridiculous, it has got nothing to do with God at all." And I can say: "As far as I am concerned this gives me some real food for thought which in my case relates to God, because I happen to be in that language or atmosphere." I don't know if this is valid, but it seems so to me.

Q When we ask God for something must it always be with the faith that we will only get it if it is his will?

We are back to petition! Do you think we can really pray to God for something that is against his will? It's a question of how deep the prayer comes from, and how much it is really prayer. The power really to pray comes from God. I mean: a lot of 'prayer' is pretty much on the surface of us, and in a way when we really pray, really ask God for things, the prayer is more likely something God is doing for us.

Q You can't always tell. It may be something you want very much.

If you are saying to God "This may not be your will but I want it just the same", I don't know theologically what happens at this point, whether you are able to change God's will. Certainly the Old Testament people seem to have been able to do it a bit, at least the way they put it suggests this; they seem to imply that God changed his mind. But I think if you wanted something which from what we understand about the nature of God must be against his will, it would not be possible. For example, if you say "please give me the opportunity to murder A, because this is the one thing I want to do", I think one might be tempted to feel that God couldn't will A's death by your hand, because it would be against his will.

Q What happens if you ask for something which isn't specifically bad, but you don't know if it is good for you or not?

Well then it will be in God's will. But you are not going to know whether in fact it is in God's will or not, are you?

Q Do you disapprove of the Maharishi and meditation?

I was not running down the Maharishi. What I was saying was that I am not doing what he is doing, but I may be wrong as I am not really clear how his meditation works. But as I understand it, his is more in terms of what I am going to discuss next time which is not so much trying to concentrate on our intellectual development in regard to what we can know about God and, from there, get that extra something which gives us a spark off. Transcendental meditation is much more developing through the use of a particular word and so going beyond one's actual intellectual faculties. But I am not very clear so it would be stupid to try to talk about it.

I was suggesting that what we call meditation seems to a lot of people to be very pedestrian and unworthwhile and not getting one far enough. Whereas the idea of transcendental meditation has captured quite a number of young minds because, at least in the beginning of the effort, it seems to take you further towards where you want to go. But still the more pedestrian sort of theme has to go on in some way or other if we are to bring our minds as well as the rest of us to God.

Q Do you think transcendental meditation differs greatly from Christian meditation?

The Christian meditational process very often tends to start on something like scripture which is really very incarnate. It is a study of the imitation of Christ or God in the world, or something like this which is going to lead you from that point of contact on earth to the Other. Whereas I think transcendental meditation would start more directly on the Other. If you start having a meditation on God you may simply be theologising or philosophising about God, rather than just taking the sense of God and holding that. I think, perhaps, this is a different way of approach. I don't know if you have to divorce the two.

Q Surely we must not stick exclusively at meditation?

What we are trying to do now is to go through a whole series of steps, stages, or types of prayer, or whatever you like to call them. So you could say at any point, if I was talking about vocal prayer, isn't there something called meditation? And when I am talking about meditation, you could say, isn't there something called contemplation? The trouble is eventually the whole of your being is going to be taken up into prayer, and insofar as you walk about, that can be prayer, and insofar as you think, that can be prayer, and insofar as you speak that can be prayer, and insofar as you go into some marvellous ecstasy that can be prayer. Eventually it is the whole thing. However, if we are going to talk about it, the only way we can do it as human beings is by making it far more systematic than in fact it is. I am not trying to cut out that aspect by this form of meditation. That is why I say at the end of one's deliberate thinking about God, one ought to be moved to a 'spiritual bouquet' or something like that, which means in one way or other you are caught up in a different sort of way in your prayer.

On Knowing and Knowing About

Somewhere in this area between meditation and more contemplative prayer, it is worth while making one or two observations which are in themselves simple and well-known, but can nevertheless elude us in their deep significance.

When we meditate, we are largely thinking about the subject. This means that we are using our mind and emotions and even senses to conjure up something as 'real to the mind'. This implies a subject outside . . . God at a distance observed and considered. It also continues to be a mental exercise, which can be enlightening, rewarding and developing of the whole person.

Supposing that you take as an example Jesus Christ. You can read about him, his origin, his family background, his place of birth. You can watch him through the Gospels, and so come to see how he reacts, what he says, the way he lives and so on. You could go deeper and seriously study his nature, human and divine.

All this and more would assist you to say: "I know quite a lot about Jesus Christ." But the problem which faces us all is whether, even when that is true, you or I can say: "I know Jesus Christ." For 'to know' is very different from 'to know about'. If you read this, and you have never met me, you cannot in honesty say you know me. But once you have met me, you can begin to say you know me, and the more often we meet, the longer our friendship, the more likely you are to be able to say with conviction if asked: "Oh yes! I know him well, or intimately or something like that." Because, you see, you will have had direct contact with me, you will have seen me, listened to me, had me listening to you, got my reactions, seen me living and all the rest.

It is surely clear that the better knowledge is the latter. 'Knowing about' is useful and normal in friendship or love, but it is not even essential then. Knowing *is* essential because you cannot really love without knowing.

Various experiences seem to me to emerge from these considerations. The most important is this: "Alright, I accept what you say about a human relationship and that in this it is more important to know than to know about. But, I do not see that I can KNOW Christ, even though I can know a lot about him." The groping answer to this Aunt Sally argument is that we move into a different language, which is the language of experience. When we are there, it is almost impossible, if not totally impossible to get across the communication barrier. Supposing for instance, you tell me that so-and-so loves you; I reply by asking how you know. You can tell me that it is obvious from his/her expression; I will say this means nothing to me. You can say that he/she wants to marry you. I say that this is not convincing to me, because lots of people have said this to me. And the discussion can go on from one point to another, with myself dismissing everything you put up as being unconvincing to me. I hazard the guess that in the end you will be forced into a corner and will say to me: "Well, it may not mean anything to you, I may not be able to convince you, but I KNOW he/she LOVES ME!"

What I am trying to get at is that there are areas of our living which are too intimate to be expressed in language, and which are so personal that the conviction I can express for myself remains totally irrelevant to you. I *know* it is true; logically you cannot follow because you are not intellectually convinced by my arguments. But the long and short is that I am totally convinced and I live as though he/she loves me. And, my word, does it not make a difference to the way I live and feel and love! Then, if I am right in what I experience of his/her love, I show the truth of it in living, not in words.

Now, with Christ, philosophers can tell me that I cannot 'know' Christ and so on. Alright, but I can still say that I am very sorry, I just do know him. And I think I can quote a backing from the Good News . . . the man born blind who had to say to his questioners: "I don't know the answer to what you are saying. All I know is that I was blind and now I see." So, also, I would feel and say of my own experience. And why not?

Next then, let us consider the developing of a

closer relationship of knowing between two people. If you are a man and you are not yet married and you see a lovely girl across the street, you may well want to come to know her. You then make the necessary moves to meet her. With luck, you strike up an acquaintance and take her out and so on. All this means you are getting to know her. (The woman reader must please transpose into the other sex!) But if you want to keep her at arm's length so that you can admire her beauty, you will never enter into a more intimate relationship. Supposing, however, you and she agree to come together into an embrace, then at the moment she goes out of your vision, you can no longer see her because she is too close, but the knowledge is altogether different because your contact with her is so much nearer.

Or take another very simple example. Hold your hand at arm's length and look at it, four fingers and a thumb and so on. Now, draw it slowly towards you. At first you can keep it in focus, and then gradually it is too close to be seen whole and clearly. Finally, it is right up against your face and you cannot see at all . . . everything is dark . . . but the contact is very real and very different. Though you cannot see, you are clear that there is something there up against your nose; you can no longer distinguish it as 'hand' or see the shape and so on. But it is very real.

Well, the same reaction occurs in relationship with God. The closer we approach, the more dark is our knowledge. It is neither easy to express this in words or to hold its credibility in life. When a person is set down before God, is trying hard to be recollected, is even trying to think of God and Christ, and all that happens is that there is a blank, an emptiness, a pain, it is not easy to get across to that person that all is well and this is as it should be! BUT IT IS AS IT SHOULD BE!

The enveloping darkness is something which is spoken of and written of all the time by those who are acknowledged 'experts' in the prayer life. I suspect that there is a certain humility, be it true or false, which invades many people who are trying to pray, by which they say; "Oh yes, I can see that this can happen to a saint or a mystic, but not to me". This becomes a good excuse which allows anything which 'I am experiencing' to be a failure on my part, a need to go back to the beginning, and a subconscious refusal to accept that God may indeed be calling me forward in darkness, weak as I am. The truth often is that I AM being called on by God and he does not mind my stupidity and weakness . . . he is only interested in me, and he wants me, if only I will let go, and not find an excuse for refusing to go on.

There follows another important and simple idea. When we meditate on 'GOD', we set our minds to think about God; we can take his omnipotence, his eternity, his omniscience and so no. We can think about them. But supposing instead of this thinking, we simply take 'GOD', we do not think about 'GOD', but we 'accept' GOD. This means that we sit or kneel there with the word and the thought and the presence of God 'with us'. There is no need for thought; there is just acceptance . . . GOD. So this word 'God' has life and being and presence. I cannot define it, I do not want to think about it; I simply want to live with the deep intangible presence —GOD.

Just in the same way as we are surrounded all the time by the atmosphere, which we think of as 'air', so with God. I go along happily breathing in this 'air', without the least thought. If I stop and try to 'catch' some air, I am frustrated, because it cannot be cupped in my hand. Normally I will not bother about that, but occasionally there will be a person who says he or she cannot breathe without touching what is breathed. An asthmatic may even need the reassurance of the hissing as well as the oxygen itself to assist his breathing because he has panicked. But ordinarily, life goes on, we breathe, we do not think about the wonder of it—yet we are dependent on air, and occasionally we might open our lungs and breathe deeply and say something like: "Thank God for fresh air!"

God is as present as the air. We do not advert to this presence, without a conscious effort, until we are trained to be sensitive to this presence. We have by that time learnt to wait openly on God without feeling that 'everything depends on me'.

From this, it is necessary to spell out a further and deeply significant matter which is readily understood once it is grasped, but may evade the ordinary man or woman at prayer. The matter is this: about ninety per cent of all prayer in a person is the work of God: only some ten per cent is the work of the person concerned. The significance of this is clearly in the fact that a great deal of time and energy is spent by people in striving for development in their prayer-life, and all the time, the most important single action is the action of God. Of course, the human being has to set himself in the way of prayer, to open himself, to get into routine and discipline in life and mentality. But far more is then due to the action of God than anyone could guess to look at the intensity and tension exhibited by quite a number who are earnest for God.

When this fact is accepted, the transition from active to passive in the life of prayer is that much easier. Our action can be seen as putting ourselves into an attitude of prayer and holding ourselves open to the Spirit. It is here again that Faith plays such a large part in the whole prayer-life, because it is probably only by faith that a person can hold himself in stillness and openness and joy, when nothing seems to happen at all. And it is at this point that the leap forward can take place, God intervening, provided that we have the courage to remain in his apparent absence and accept his presence, until such times as he makes it clear to us that this is worth while. Mind you, this is not easy, and it does take quite a lot of self-discipline, patience and the humility of accepting being blankly stupid.

Quickly or slowly, but certainly surely, the Spirit will invade and take over, in a darkness which has been described as dazzling, in the white light of radiant joy, in the stillness of complete tranquillity. It is at this meeting point, that the person can subsequently refer to a moment of truth, and can call upon the experience to justify his assertion that he 'knows God' in the sense of 'experiencing God', no matter what contrary argument is put forward on rational, philosophical or other grounds. Indeed, if he is asked to explain what he means by the assertion, he may well become tongue-tied and totally ineffective except in his sincerity and integrity. What he has done is to follow the 'stupid' advice of Christ to his fishermen disciples who had laboured all night and caught nothing . . . "Launch out into the deep and let down your nets for the catch". Mad, mad, mad . . . but it works!

I think perhaps I must also say here that 'being with' or 'being in the presence of' are very important attitudes. The disciples were with Jesus. I cannot be with him in the same way, but by insisting on setting aside myself and my time, often alone in human terms, I make myself as available as I may. Then I try to remain there in a state of openness, unworried by thoughts or philosophies, not bothered about distractions, and happy to be with the one I know and love—not knowing if I know and therefore loving in a way I do not understand, but experiencing without understanding it. It is real but not explicable!

Experience of deeper involvement

If we are going to learn about prayer ourselves and to be ready to talk to other people about it, we have got to be prepared to accept that there are very many ways of coming to know, love and serve God; and that, if we can learn more about them, we are going to be of more use to other people. This after all is part of the active apostolic side of prayer, for it is not something we do simply for ourselves. From prayer (which is the union of ourselves with God) comes salvation and perfection which is what he wants for us, and for the whole world.

How you and I may be able to effect this with God, will depend on the degree that we have opened ourselves to him. In doing this, we are children and like children we all have our own approaches. We invent our own games as it were, and there aren't always rules unless we make them up. To some extent prayer is the game that is made up between us and God. In the same kind of way that two people deeply in love with each other have their own names for things, for each other and other people, and may invent their own language which is almost incommunicable to others, so it can happen between us and God. Therefore talking about the further levels and depths of prayer is very individual and yet a certain common theme or strand runs through it, which does mean something to other people.

We are going on now to discuss contemplation. And to see what has been said about this way I will give extracts from three mystical authors. First, *The Cloud of Unknowing*:

> 'Lift up thine heart unto God with a meek stirring of love, and mean himself and none of his goods. And thereto look that thou loathe to think on aught but himself, so that nought work in thy mind nor thy will but only himself. And do that in thee is to forget all the creatures that God ever made and the works of them, so that thy thought or thy desire be not directed or stretched to any of them, neither in general nor in special.'[1]

This is the beginning of the active putting away of one's thought. Then Walter Hilton:

> 'When a man perceives the love of this world false and failing . . . he may not at once feel the love of God, but he must abide a while in the night for he may not suddenly come from that one light to that other, that is from the love of the world to the perfect love of God. This night is naught else but a forbearing and a withdrawing of the thought of the soul from earthly things by great desire and yearning for to love and see and feel Jesu and ghostly things.'[2]

[1] *Cloud of Unknowing*, chap. 3, p. 7f., ed. Justin McCann, Burns Oates, 1924.

[2] Walter Hilton, *Scale of Perfection*, Book II, chap. 24, ed. Gerard Sitwell, p. 205, Burns Oates, 1955, ed. Evelyn Underhill, p. 321, Watkins, 1948.

Hilton is again saying the same sort of thing. The last quotation on this is from Saint John of the Cross:

> 'For God's sake they are now able to suffer a light burden and a little aridity without turning back to a time which they found more pleasant. When they are going about these spiritual exercises with the greatest delight and pleasure, and when they believe the sun of Divine favour is shining most brightly upon them. God turns all this light of theirs into darkness, and shuts against them the door and the source of sweet spiritual water which they were tasting in God . . . And thus he leaves them so completely in the dark that they know not whither to go with their sensible imagination and meditation; for they cannot advance a step in meditation . . . their inward senses being submerged in this night and left with such dryness that not only do they experience no pleasure and consolation in spiritual things and good exercises wherein they were wont to find their delight and pleasures, but instead they find insipidity and bitterness in the said things . . . God (now) sets them down from His arms and teaches them to walk on their own feet; which they feel to be very strange, for everything seems to be going wrong with them.'[3]

One could produce many other quotations of this sort. It would seem therefore that there should be in the individual a development in which the thought, the imagination, the understanding and so on in one way or another seem to grow more or less useless. This can happen perhaps at the beginning of one's

---

[3] *Dark Night of the Soul*, Book I, chap. 8, trans E. Allison Peers, Burns Oates, 1957.

prayer, perhaps mid-way, or perhaps after a long series of dry meditations; one cannot tell when. It depends on the individual. At this particular point there is a tendency to think that one must go back and start again and to say to oneself: "I've made a muck of this. I used to have good thoughts and now I am terribly distracted." We can make a tremendous business of trying desperately hard and as a result probably become all tensed up. Now at this stage, if you have courage, you must 'launch out into the deep' as Christ said to the apostles when they were about to go fishing. So deliberately 'launch out into the deep,' and quite actively begin putting aside these thoughts which at other times of the day are perfectly good. At the time when you are close to God in your own prayer, try actively not to meditate or think about God in the ways that you have done previously. This is one way of doing it.

And though it is not necessarily essential, it is quite useful to try to still the imagination by attempting to concentrate by using one word or a short phrase and to give yourself in an active sort of way, in an active abandonment to God with the increased realisation of the uselessness of your understanding or intelligence. This is, however, something that is not altogether acceptable to the whole of you because part of you is going to be very irritated by it and will want to get hold of things and think them out, whilst another part of you is going to get attracted by imaginations. Sometimes there will be a certain unease about it, and one part of you will fight against another part. Little devils, imaginations or what have you, will creep in and say "This is nonsense", "This is absurd", "This is a waste of time, get on and do something proper and don't hang about like this". And if it grows and develops as it should do, it will be then something that you get yourself trained into to some extent, that is by going through with the active part of it. You hold yourself there and you are determined not to get up and run away, though you may want to do this. The seeming uselessness of it becomes something that you are more able to bear.

This is for some people a time where considerable asceticism is needed because it seems that somehow or other I must give myself more to God. I must somehow or other get away from all the encumbrances, and I want therefore to do penance, I want to fast, to spend long hours in prayer, and I want therefore to chastise the body, and so on. This may be a phase people will go through at this stage all in a natural desire to purge and purify themselves so as to come closer to the One whom one loves. In the prayer time itself the adverse reactions still continue because it is very difficult to remain in this darkness and in this lack of anything for the senses to grasp on to.

Also you have at a certain level, perhaps, a dull ache, a certain emptying for which you are partially responsible for you are casting things out of your mind, but this leaves an emptiness that is partly a longing and sometimes partly a frustration, and partly a rebellion even, all mingled together. It can become an active pain in you, and it can have some strange effects on you sometimes because it is possible for you both now and in the later stages to become very abstracted outside prayer. This does happen to people in this stage of contemplation. You suddenly find yourself, for example, dropping things, forgetting things, or you get stuck in the middle of a sentence and wonder what you were saying. A strange kind of dichotomy can occur. This can be quite embarrassing for some people as the reality of the world, which is now to some extent alien, still presses forward and the two can clash. It can be quite a difficult problem.

I have explained before, but I want to state it here again, that what is happening at this stage is that one is becoming more aware of the fact that God is too vast, too immense for one, and therefore one is unable to comprehend him; one is closer to him (though these words don't mean anything) and so one is too close to see the whole of him and to understand him by any of the means we normally use, and out of this comes darkness, flatness.

All this is explained rather better in *The Cloud of Unknowing*. For example the author writes: "I find this but a darkness, and as it were a cloud of unknowing, thou knowest not what, saving that thou feelest in thy will a naked intent unto God. This darkness and this cloud . . . hindereth thee so that thou mayest neither see Him clearly by light of understanding in thy reason, nor feel Him in sweetness of love in thine affection. And therefore shape thee to bide in this darkness . . . as long as thou mayest ever more crying after Him whom thou lovest. For if ever thou shall see Him and feel Him as it be here, it must always be in this cloud and in this darkness"[1] . . . "smite upon that thick cloud of unknowing with a sharp dart of longing love."[2] And gradually or suddenly, or—I don't know what to say, this becomes something which is more passive. And the important thing about the passive, of course, is that it is passive. By that I mean there is a swing from even consciously trying to put things away.

[1] *Cloud of Unknowing*, Chap. 3.
[2] Op. cit. Chap. 6.

Now, and this happens almost unconsciously, you no longer have consciously to put things away but rather it begins to happen in you. When I say 'it' I mean the Spirit of God, who begins to work in you so that you are really sitting there, kneeling there, standing there, being there. Of yourself you can't make yourself aware of God, all you can do is to be there in the place that God is. But you are not even conscious of the fact that God is. So what are you conscious of? I don't know what you are conscious of because, perhaps, you are not conscious of anything at all. Sometimes you may be.

Sometimes, as the *Cloud of Unknowing* says you feel yourself to be a lump of sin, and there is just a tremendous sense of emptiness and sinfulness in oneself and one is somehow caught into the whole sin of the world. At other times one is just conscious of God in some way, but one is not clear how, or one is similarly conscious of love. Sometimes there seems to be no consciousness at all— one just is. Other times there can be a very desolate state, and not just an arid but a tremendous pain, which seems almost to be a complete alienation of yourself from everything that is good. There is nothing you can do about it. You can't move it. You can't take hold of either the pain, the joy or the love that may be in it. It isn't something you can take hold of, it just is, and you are there in it.

A lot of the time, and time is the thing that one measures by, I suppose, there just isn't anything at all in a strange way. One is simply there. All this does grow and develop without one realising that it grows and develops. And this is one of the reasons why it is very important to have someone who is, as it were, behind you or alongside you and able to help you with this, because it is a completely uncharted route. You don't even know if you are coming or going, you don't know if you are going backwards or forwards. At least this is not quite true as part of you does know. But it is necessary to have some human reassurance because it does seem to be so strange.

The strangeness of it is that you do know, but you don't know through your ordinary intellect or through your understanding. I don't know what words one uses about this. Simply one is aware of it without having been told about it or having worked it out in one's own mind, or without having said that is so. It is just God's working upon you in such a way that, even without knowing that you know, something happens and goes on happening to you, and produces various developments and fruits in your life.

Time: sometimes time doesn't pass at all, because this state of passive contemplation, if one can call it that, is not something which is by any means necessarily continuous. And therefore perhaps the difficulty of it is, in a way, that one is never quite clear whether it is there or not. Sometimes it will take a couple of hours to get through five minutes, and it is as flighty as this, one might say. It happens like this I suppose, because God needs to work on us in different ways and needs to purify us from time to time.

Also he sometimes puts us through a certain amount of the agony of man, through the agony of man growing closer to the godhead, and the agony of man understanding in the depth of his being as he has never understood before what the might and power of God is, so that he is literally awestruck by it. And at another time we may have to face sin in a way we have never quite faced it before, not seeing it as telling a lie or murdering somebody, but just as sheer agony which is indescribable. It is only perhaps afterwards that you can say I now know something of what sin is or of what sin does. At the time, however, you did not recognise it and could perhaps hardly endure it.

Joy: that comes very often when time passes like nothing on earth, because it is so indescribable just to be there and not to be there. It just is indescribable, so that you almost feel yourself bursting out of yourself. But a very great deal of the time, as I know it, is simply being there, and neither being particularly hot nor cold, neither being bright nor dull, being grey perhaps, being completely idle, not knowing at all if God is communicating but simply being there in faith. It may mean keeping yourself there in a more active way by making an occasional ejaculation of love and faith. The human side will continually come back and say quite straightly, 'you are being a bloody fool, for heaven's sake get up and do something active'. Not only will you say that but your friends will say it too. They will say, 'What on earth are you wasting time on that sort of thing for? Don't you realise all that sort of nonsense is out now? The only thing you can possibly do is to go out and help your neighbour. This is a waste of time, you are being self-indulgent. This is a psychiatric malaise you have got', and one thing or another of this sort. People are not slow to say this.

There is, therefore, necessarily in this a considerable amount of suffering, and this is all part of the dying to oneself in order that one can live to Christ. And I think because of the way that God continues to work in one, even though one can't sense it, a sensitivity which is very much a universal sensitivity, begins to emerge and grow out of this union, this closeness with God. It is a sensitivity to the pain of the world, to the care of the world, to the universality of mankind in relation to God. This should, I am sure, if God is working in one in the full way, open one up more and more to one's neighbour. One might say the proof of the pudding is whether or not it does do this. If it does not, it may be that you are just deceiving yourself.

I must give a clear word of warning about this, and this is where we differ quite largely from some other persuasions: contemplation is not a state of perfection. You are never going to be perfect in the complete sense until you are in the next world, and so you are still subject to imperfection, though you are able to be contemplative in an active and passive way. The general thesis, however, would be that you are not going to be able to be in a really close relationship with God in this way and then be constantly dashing off and murdering people in your spare time, because the two things are too incompatible. But since you are still a human being, you are still going to get ratty, still going to get tired, still going to be ill, and perhaps even some of your faults are going to seem to be much greater than they were before. Contemplation is not something which is going to make you into a perfect paragon straight away, as far as everyone else is concerned. However, I think it is true to say that a certain tranquillity does pervade, and that there is a certain sense of depth, a sureness and peace. These sort of things are definitely to be found in a contemplative person.

I am not going to talk about visions and revelations and thing like that, for the simple reason that I don't know anything about them. All I would say is that somehow visions and revelations are not necessary in the way that they are sometimes suggested to be, because the whole thing is in a sense a vision. The world looks different. People look different. God looks different. The senses are different. Therefore, I suppose in one way it could be said that in the deepness and fullness of contemplative prayer when it is experienced, there is something of revelation, of light, though it is something that is inexpressible because I think the very language, the image and so on, is not a worded one. So where you get someone like Saint John of the Cross, or *The Cloud of Unknowing*, trying to tell of the revelation of Divine love, the words which are used are after-thoughts and in a sense almost rationalisations, memories in tranquillity perhaps, but they are not the reality.

It is very difficult to look at the writings of someone like Saint John of the Cross or another mystical author and see anything other than signs and pointers towards something which for you must be a direct real experience. This means too that quite often it is not easy to express it afterwards except as someone like Saint John of the Cross might do in a rather codified, classified way with steps and stages, because somehow or other perhaps he feels he has got to do it so that people can follow him. Yet it probably does not happen in this way, it is not nearly so cut and dried, and easy to delimit. The active and the passive flow in and out of each other, and the contemplative, the vocal and the meditative flow in and out of each other, because as I have said to you before, and I must reiterate, it becomes life, and life becomes it, and it is this constant sense of communication with, companionship with, union with the One, with the Trinity, with God, with Christ.

It does not matter which way you look at it or which way it strikes you. In fact it may not strike you in any of these ways particularly. It is, nevertheless, a reality that will have its different depths at different times of the day, and different states of your life. You are not the master of your own being any longer in a certain sense, because you don't know how God is going to take you, or when he is going to take you, or where he is going to take you. This itself is very interesting, because out of your powerlessness, there has to grow a certain amount of humility because anything that you say seems so utterly stupid and futile in regard to what you are trying to say and trying to put across to people. The advice you give seems to be tremendously banal, and the way of living seems very stupid, and you get an increasing sense of your own stupidity and worthlessness, and uselessness. But at the same time, out of the corner of your eye as it were, you can see things happening which are very peculiar indeed and seem to have no relation to yourself because, just as with your prayer there is no understanding of where all this came from.

I would like to end by saying this: I think everybody can come to the point of active contemplation in which you can deliberately set yourselves down before God and, as it were, open your minds to him, and train yourself to be there open to him. This itself is something I am sure that everyone should come to do because it is going further than the meditative, and sometimes rather shallow, workings of one's own intellect. One can in this opening up, at least, leave oneself in the position where it is up to God to do what he wants to do. It seems to some people that nothing ever does happen. Some almost get stuck at that point and they think, or it looks as though God does not ever treat them as passive instruments of his love. It may be that they are not sufficiently sensitive, but I think at this point there is not anything that one can do except be there. Therefore faithfulness is quite the most important thing.

So if you can, and I think this applies to every single one of you, put yourself there in front of God in this actively contemplative state, if one can call it that. And after that the whole question is, have you the strength, the guts, the regularity, the perseverance, the humility, the openness—you can go endlessly saying the things that you ought to have —to leave yourself there constantly in the presence of God, day in and day out, and night in and night out, though nothing seems to be happening. If you have got that then of course I cannot lay down what God will do to you, but it seems to me likely that in the course of time, you will either be told by your director, or may come to sense it yourself that God is working in you and that you are in a passive way a contemplative too.

But of course it is a way of life, and it is a way of life that is not incompatible with intense activity; it is not incompatible with marriage, it is not incompatible at all with a family or with any form of life that I know. Clearly some forms of life can be very much more difficult for it. For example if the person is too active or the mind is too active it will be harder. The amount of active contemplation (that is setting yourself aside a time, a place and a silence for this sort of beginning) becomes more important the fuller your life is. The emptier your life is, the more you need to regulate your emptiness into positive periods for God. It is very easy in an empty life to let emptiness pervade everything and gradually one's whole being becomes empty. So it is useful to find someone who can help you on this.

Contemplation and the way of life it involves is very demanding, but it is worth all the risks, the pain, the struggles, the hard work it may entail for by it the love of God can grow and work in us in a most wonderful and all-embracing way.

Q The average individual does not practise prayer in the way that you have just described. It seems like a psychological ploy, or a kind of Christian Yoga. It seems a way of tranquillising oneself rather than anything positive.

This is the very thing about it; because it is passive all your hackles will rise and you will find all kinds of reasons against it, like comparing it to Yoga, or saying that it is a psychological ploy. In fact I think I suggested that this is the sort of thing you would be attacked for. I can only say to you, find a contemplative and see what he or she is up to, and if you can genuinely say "yes here it is, this person is neurotic and just sitting down and letting the world go by", then well and good. But the contemplatives that I have met are just not like this.

However, I do not know how I can get this across. All I can say is, if you have an instinct for it, you must pursue it. I do not think that it is necessarily very easy to sell this to people. To some extent you can sell transcendental meditation because people have to begin with a tremendous sort of discipline, and this is something they can do. As long as it is like this, it is marvellous, but when you just have to sit there, it is not nearly so marvellous and that is the time when the Beatles get up and go home. But I do not think that I can explain it better than that, or give you any other reassurance.

Q Is contemplation to be regarded and pursued as an end in itself, or is it to be seen as something that makes you more active and efficient?

You are not pursuing contemplation, you are pursuing God, and God is pursuing you. The difficulty is that you do not really know what God is going to get at with you. But it seems to be, from the fruit as it were, that a person lives more fully. And this living more fully is first and foremost, though inexplicably, having some deeper knowledge, love, awareness of God, and the effect of this seems to be to send people out into the world to get on with things. I suppose it is as it were, good diffusing itself or something of this sort.

Q You say God sends people out into the world. Do you mean that they become more active?

Yes, partly I do—God in you drives you out to others. I imagine active for you means going out and doing something for somebody. But there is another aspect; you can be active for God, at least this would be my theory, simply in suffering or something like this. You can be active for God in concern in a strange way by simply being who you are where you are, because you cannot tell at all what is coming out of you. But it is not easy to pin down because each person is different.

What I am really trying to put across is that a contemplative is not necessarily just sitting in a monastery, or on an island, or alone somewhere, though this is one of the forms God has of using people. Sometimes also these people are used because they find themselves needing to write about it, or sometimes people are drawn to them, and they become known by just being there. Sometimes as in the case of Saint Dominic activity occurs in a different way in preaching and in going out in missionary work. Then look at Saint Benedict: he took himself right away out of Rome, out of the worldliness in order to find God, and spent his time at Subiaco alone in contemplation, and then from this, there grew around him a whole body of people who learned from him about contemplation. And out of this grew the most extraordinary civilising, educating process in the Western world. You cannot tell how the thing is going to work. Perhaps, sometimes we tend to look at it in a too short term way.

Q Is not contemplation always having God in your mind and being with him wherever you are, and whatever you are doing, for even though you don't feel him you know that he is there?

It is difficult to express it in words. In a sense we each have our own language about it and we can talk about it best in terms of the way we know it. So it is quite useful for individuals to talk to others about it, because they may suddenly find something strikes a spark with them, something that they have also experienced. I think I have described it before in terms of being in love with somebody when your first waking consciousness is one of joy, even before you realise what it is. Then later you realise on waking more, that you are deeply in love with this person. In a certain sense this remains true of the whole of one's life with God, though there may be other times when you wake up with a sense of agony.

When I say wake up it does not need to be waking up from sleep. It just overwhelms you at some stages and you cannot think why, what or how, because the level, putting it in ordinary mundane terms, of being in love with God is something that goes through the whole of your life. Sometimes his absence is so intense that it is as though he had died, or had given up loving you, or you feel that you might have given up loving him. At other times, particularly when you are concentrated in the sense that you have put yourself there, he can take hold of you, but equally he can take hold of you at any other time, rather in the same way you cannot tell exactly how your love for another person is going to rise or fall at any particular stage. The very talking about it and analysing it in a way begins to make it seem unreal or strange, but it is very real when it happens.

The Spirit moving among us

Though this chapter may seem slightly different from the ones which have gone before, I think you will realise as you come through it that there is a union between them. And you will perhaps also see that the seeming difference is one which has been present among the people of God over the ages. The Spirit blows where he wills, and this is not always in the direction which church leaders might expect or think right. But it is surely deep in tradition that the Spirit cannot be confined or regulated, and where lines are drawn and limits set down somehow he no longer manifests himself.

What is interesting today is the gradual rediscovery of the Spirit in the Churches. Beginning in Evangelical Protestantism in USA it has even penetrated the Roman Catholic church at this time. I am not intending to attempt to write on Pentecostalism because my knowledge and experience is neither so clear or so vivid as others who have already written balanced and embracing accounts.

There are, however, a few things which in my amateur way I can say, in the hope that it will help some of those who are naturally too inhibited to open up, and encourage some of those who are doubtful and unsure to take the plunge of at least asking for the growth-realisation of the Spirit in themselves.

As with the development of prayer in the life of ordinary people, where we have tended to be scared either of going too far ourselves or allowing others to go too far, so with the realisation of the place of the Spirit in Christian living. 'Union with Christ', 'Christ living in us' and the 'Gift of the Spirit' are, if I am right to put it that way, the birthright of the Christian, with the sacrament of baptism being the birth. So, they are not just for the select few Christians, but for all those who are born again 'of water and the Holy Spirit' through the sacrament. The only stipulation, perhaps, is that the Christian after initiation has his part to play in the development of the human and divine, in himself and in the world. If he does not respond, does not want to respond and does not lay himself open to the emergence of the Spirit in him, practically nothing will happen. But if he is willing, this willingness brings the Spirit into fuller being in him, and he has the opportunity of showing his great love and desire in receiving the Body and Blood of Christ in the Eucharist any and all days of the week. So the economy of God in the growth of Christ and the Spirit in man is dependent on man's part.

In our 'respectable religious approach', we have often implied that somehow it is not quite nice to ask for the Spirit to be manifest in us, though we have cultivated petitionary prayer in the most mundane areas of our living. Surely, in asking for the development of the final end of our whole being, for which God has created us we are no less likely to receive the answer to our prayer. "Come Holy Spirit and fill the hearts of the faithful. Kindle in them the fire of your love. . . ." This ancient prayer has been said so many times, but I have the sad feeling that the general sense has been that we are not really expecting the Holy Spirit to come and would be rather dismayed if he did take us at our word.

But our 'conversion' must begin with praying from our heart's depth and really wanting the outcome of our prayer, without any holds barred or limits set. Open up!

Christ himself says: "I will ask the Father and he will give you another helper, the Spirit of truth, to stay with you forever. The world cannot receive him, because it cannot see him or know him. But you know him, for he remains with you and lives with you." (John 14:16–17). Then he tells them: "Wait for the gift my Father promised, that I told you about" and their response was: "They all joined together in a group to pray frequently" (Acts 1:4 and 14).

We would do well then in our growth in Christ to ask for and seek the Spirit in our lives, singly and together. Notice I deliberately say 'seek the Spirit IN our lives'. He does not have to come again. Scripturally and traditionally there is strong backing, and though more recently there has been a wariness about 'movements of the Spirit' because of fear of excess, and though there is always a danger of 'enthusiasm' rather than openness to the working of the Spirit, there is such a need for the rebirth of the Spirit in the Church of today that I am quite thoughtfully urging you to let drop your inhibitions and your caution . . . let us go forward hoping and praying for the New Pentecost prayed for by Pope John XXIII.

I have mentioned the Spirit in previous chapters. It is he who works in us: "When the Spirit of truth comes, he will lead you into all truth. . . . He will give me glory, for he will take what I have to say and tell it to you." (John 16:13 and 14). It is he who prays in us: "The Spirit makes you God's sons, and by the Spirit's power we cry to God, 'Father, Father'. God's Spirit joins himself to our spirits to declare we are God's children." (Romans 8:15–16). It is he who lives in us: "Those who live as the Spirit tells them to live, have their minds controlled by what the Spirit wants. . . . But you do not live as your human nature tells you to; you live as the Spirit tells you to—if, in fact God's Spirit lives in you. Whoever does not have the Spirit of Christ does not belong to him." (Romans 8:5 and 9).

To me one of the very straight, simple passages of the Gospel which we all believe and ignore is Christ's promise: "Whoever loves me will obey my message. My Father will love him, and my Father and I will come to him and live with him. . . . The helper, the Holy Spirit whom the Father will send in my name, will teach you everything, and make you remember all I have told you" (John 14:23 and 26).

This is true for us today, for you and for me. Come then, let it be your personal task to open yourself to the realisation that God is with you, in you, that you are the temple of the Holy Spirit, that you can really recognise Christ in your fellow men because Christ is really there.

To put yourself into the way of realisation in full faith and hope that this will come about is your part in co-operating in the work of the Spirit. We are often nervous of 'conversion', and we are right to be when it appears to be self-induced as an emotional response. This is very different in kind from the realisation of the Spirit which brings love, peace, patience. We must not ignore that the Spirit really does 'come to birth' in a person who has received the Spirit at Baptism . . . but in different ways. He 'blows where he will', and this means the emergence may be a slow process, only realised in hindsight, or a sudden flowering, or the hidden growth of well-sown seed.

Perhaps a deeper and happier acceptance of the presence and working of the Spirit would ease the acceptance of growth in prayer.

This is the point at which to make it clear that very few go forward in the Spirit alone. Normally there is help from outside . . . book, preacher, confessor, friend, spiritual guide or director. This is part of our inter-dependence as men and women; it is also part of the humility necessary for the manifestation of the true Spirit. He seems to demand in us a surrender and an exposure, where our poverty, dirtiness, inadequacy and the rest surface to the gaze of another. And at this juncture, a "brother helping a brother is like a strong fortress".

From here, it is such a small and logical step to group prayer, yet it seems for some to be equivalent to the 'small step' of the first astronaut onto the Moon. All the inhibitions and shyness rear up in some people at the very idea; yet there is a thoroughly scriptural basis. Often quoted is Christ's: "Where two or three are gathered together in my name, I am there with them" (Matt. 18:20): there is the example of the apostles before Pentecost, already quoted, and so on. But we are often shy of 'letting go' in public; the thought of sitting together prayerfully, silently, perhaps emptily, waiting to be moved by the Spirit, to say something over which you really have minimal control . . . well many excuses can be found to put off such a scary moment!

However, it is my experience in common with others that it is possible to lead and encourage ordinary people, men and women, old and young into group prayer. The outcome growth is remarkable. Of course, there is 'sales-resistance', because the whole idea may be alien to the way of life and prayer in which they have been taught to grow up from childhood. If you are in this category, do not be surprised at yourself resisting, but also make the effort of will necessary to try openness. Fear rules our hearts.

But the Lord himself found that he terrified his followers, and he had to encourage them by saying: "Fear not, it is I". And the reaction to his action was Peter's response: "Depart from me, because I am a sinful man." If, then, you are afraid, take courage, and "launch out into the deep."

If you have not gone forward in the Spirit, it may be surprising to you that when you have you will be able to do things in the Spirit which you either could not do before, or did not have the guts to do. I am not speaking now of the use of tongues or of healing, but of the simple things like unbuttoning, losing fear, losing self-consciousness in public, being encouraged to pray, willing to communicate the Spirit to others, where before your religion was really very private; false humility emerging into true humility. If the Spirit sometimes makes us seem fools or mad, he also removes a lot of that self-consciousness which makes us curl up into our shell as a natural reaction to being exposed.

Once we can begin to glimpse the purpose of coming together for prayer, it becomes clear that our sharing adds cumulative power. Not only do we get warmth and strength from the gathering in the Spirit, but we gain courage both from our weakness, and the strength of those others who are with us, and we give others courage in the Spirit by our weakness and strength. And later, we share insights and gain insights and give insights in the Spirit, going into a new understanding which we did not know we could reach. The mingling of the flames of two candles grow bigger into one, and shed more light.

Then in this situation it is not uncommon to experience the need to pray for a particular individual in the group or outside it, who has not yet 'come alive' in the Spirit. As with anything which we experience as good and lovely and true we wish to share it, so now we wish to share the Spirit.

It may seem strange that it is now that physical contact can become the obvious means of communication. Sometimes to sit or stand in prayer or singing, holding hands, is not just a gimmick or an emotive trick, but it is a genuine, deep assurance of unity in the Spirit. So too, the laying on of hands is at this point a simple, meaningful and effective gesture for the sharing of the Spirit.

I find it to be true that this coming together in the Spirit is proved by its fruits. Those who do so enter into a new phase or mode of being. It is not easily described—but it can be known. It induces an assurance, a tranquillity, a new depth of faith, and outwardly-looking a new usefulness spiritually for the rest of the world. It would be silly and wrong to give the impression that from henceforward they 'live happily ever after'. Christ does not take us out of the world; he wishes us to continue along the way of the Cross, through Calvary, to the Resurrection.

But the paradox is that while going along the road to Jerusalem we are also living in the Resurrection and in Pentecost through our baptism. In theology and in reason it is very difficult to grasp how Christ the God-man exists in this life on earth and supports the two natures without doing damage to one or other; the all-knowing God in human nature having a limited knowledge; the all powerful God in human nature limited to earthly-physical development; the everlasting God in his human nature dying. I am no theologian; I put these points crudely—I hope not heretically—but this is a problem of co-existence.

For one who is living Christianity, not by his own strength and power, but in a co-operating openness with the Holy Spirit, there is experience which touches the possibility of understanding. I simply mean by this that the awareness is in two dimensions: "I am an unprofitable servant" and also "his grace in me has not been void" (I Cor. 15:10). The fully living Christian is fully living this apparent contradiction. I do not pretend to be able to put into words this paradox . . . but that it is true in life I KNOW. It is seen in the radiance of a terribly suffering person's peace; in the cutting insight of an unschooled Christian, in the amazing grace of one who is converted and convinced in facing the rationally compelling arguments of a non-believer.

Now, the long and short of all this is that there are probably in your life vast areas of undiscovered growth in the Spirit. If, in fact, you already know what I am talking about then this is an incentive to go out and do more about growing and developing.

In many ways we are in the situation of the disciples when Christ said to them: "My food is to obey the will of him who sent me and finish the work he gave me to do. . . . I tell you take a good look at the fields: the crops are now ripe and ready to be harvested; the man who reaps the crop is being paid and gathers the harvest for eternal life; so that the man who plants and the man who reaps will be glad together" (John 4:34 to 36).

Let us then be glad and rejoice for the kingdom of God is at hand. And let the only possible prayer be always on our lips . . . "Come, Lord Jesus!"

THE ONE WHO LISTENS: A BOOK OF PRAYER

paper 2.25

By Rev. Michael Hollings and Etta Gullick. This is a prayer book, a glimpse into man's dialogue with "the One Who listens." All of us are at a loss for words with which to pray, at times, and rely upon the Spirit within to express our plea. Here the Spirit speaks through men and women of the past (St. John of the Cross, Thomas More, Dietrich Bonhoeffer), and present (Michael Quoist, Mother Teresa, Malcolm Boyd). There are also prayers from men of other faiths such as Muhammed and Tagore.

God meets us where we are and since men share in sorrow, joy and anxiety, *their* prayers are *our* prayers. This is a book that will be outworn, perhaps, but never outgrown.

SEEKING PURITY OF HEART: THE GIFT OF OURSELVES TO GOD

illus 1.25

By Joseph Breault. For those of us who feel that we do not live up to God's calling, that we have sin of whatever shade within our hearts. This book shows how we can begin a journey which will lead from our personal darkness to wholeness in Christ's light — a purity of heart. Clear, practical help is given us in the constant struggle to free ourselves from the deceptions that sin has planted along all avenues of our lives.

DISCOVERING PATHWAYS TO PRAYER

paper 1.75

By. Msgr. David E. Rosage. The moment we experience prayer as "a gift" we are caught in surprise. So begins a joyous awakening, a wondrous miracle, the revelation of which tells us: following Jesus was never meant to be dull, or worse, just duty-filled.

Those who would aspire to a life of prayer and those who have already begun, will find Msgr. Rosage's *Discovering Pathways to Prayer* amazingly thorough in its scripture-punctuated approach.

"A simple but profound book which explains the many ways and forms of prayer by which the person hungering for closer union with God may find him."
Emmanuel Spillane, O.C.S.O., Abbott, Our Lady of the Holy Trinity Abbey, Huntsville, Utah

Order from your bookstore or
LIVING FLAME PRESS, Locust Valley, N.Y. 11560

PROMPTED BY THE SPIRIT 2.25

By Rev. Paul Sauvé. A handbook by a Catholic Charismatic Renewal national leader for all seriously concerned about the future of the renewal and interested in finding answers to some of the problems that have surfaced in small or large prayer groups. It is a call to all Christians to find answers with the help of a wise Church tradition as transmitted by her ordained ministers. The author has also written *Petals of Prayer/Creative Ways to Pray.*

PETALS OF PRAYER: Creative Ways To Pray

By Rev. Paul Sauvé 1.50

"*Petals of Prayer is an extremely practical book for anyone who desires to pray but has difficulty finding a method for so doing. At least 15 different methods of prayer are described and illustrated in simple, straightforward ways, showing they can be contemporary even though many of them enjoy a tradition of hundreds of years. In an excellent introductory chapter, Fr. Sauvé states that the best 'method' of prayer is the one which unites us to God. . . . Father Sauvé masterfully shows how traditional methods of prayer can be very much in tune with a renewed church.*"
St. Anthony Messenger

CRISIS OF FAITH
Invitation to Christian Maturity 1.50

By Rev. Thomas Keating, ocso. How to hear ourselves called to discipleship in the Gospels is Abbot Thomas' important and engrossing message. As Our Lord forms His disciples, and deals with His friends or with those who come asking for help in the Gospels, we can receive insights into the way He is forming or dealing with us in our day to day lives.

IN GOD'S PROVIDENCE:
The Birth of a Catholic Charismatic Parish 1.25

By Rev. John Randall. The engrossing story of the now well-known Word of God Prayer Community in St. Patrick's Parish, Providence, R.I. as it developed from Father Randall's first adverse reaction to the budding Charismatic Movement to today as it copes with the problems of being a truly pioneer Catholic Charismatic Parish.

**Order from your bookstore or
LIVING FLAME PRESS, Locust Valley, N.Y. 11560**

Books by Venard Polusney, O. Carm.

UNION WITH THE LORD IN PRAYER
Beyond Meditation To Affective Prayer Aspiration And Contemplation .85

"A magnificent piece of work. It touches on all the essential points of Contemplative Prayer. Yet it brings such a sublime subject down to the level of comprehension of the 'man in the street,' and in such an encouraging way."
Abbott James Fox, O.C.S.O. (former superior of Thomas Merton at the Abbey of Gethsemani)

ATTAINING SPIRITUAL MATURITY FOR CONTEMPLATION (According to St. John of the Cross) .85

"I heartily recommend this work with great joy that at last the sublime teachings of St. John of the Cross have been brought down to the understanding of the ordinary Christian without at the same time watering them down. For all (particularly for charismatic Christians) hungry for greater contemplation."
Rev. George A Maloney, S.J., Editor of Diakonia, Professor of Patristics and Spirituality, Fordham University.

THE PRAYER OF LOVE ... THE ART OF ASPIRATION
1.50

"It is the best book I have read which evokes the simple and loving response to remain in love with the Lover. To read it meditatively, to imbibe its message of love, is to have it touch your life and become part of what you are."
Mother Dorothy Guilbault, O. Carm., Superior General, Lacombe, La.

From the writings of John of St. Samson, O. Carm., mystic and charismatic

PRAYER, ASPIRATION AND CONTEMPLATION
Translated and edited by Venard Poslusney, O. Carm. Paper 3.95

All who seek help in the exciting journey toward contemplation will find in these writings of John of St. Samson a compelling inspiration and support along with the practical guidance needed by those who travel the road of prayer.

**Order from your bookstore or
LIVING FLAME PRESS, Locust Valley, N.Y. 11560**